THE LAND OF THE BRAVE

Wah-pi-koo Mahtoo Kalee, in His Wanth

Ne gau ru au gele	Ie gous har aee	Tehi cue depe	Ita cite	Uotau gele	Semsng ga	Ne gui e el unfrane
Beaver	Stiki hee	TwoGuns	Steep Rock	Black Squirrel	Long Horns The Chief	Little Bear

Lithograph by Denis Dighton (Cat. no. 50)

ii

THE LAND OF THE BRAVE

The North American Indian collection in the Ulster Museum, Belfast

Winifred Glover

Photographs by Bill Porter

Blackstaff Press

Published by Blackstaff Press Limited, 255A Upper Newtownards Road, Belfast BT4 3JF.

ISBN 0 85640 118 8

Printed in Northern Ireland by Belfast Litho Printers Limited.

CONTENTS

NORTHWEST
COAST

SUBARCTIC

EASTERN
WOODLANDS

PLAINS

FAR WEST

SOUTH WEST

SOUTHEAST

THE INDIAN TRIBES OF NORTH AMERICA

Subarctic
1. Kutchin
2. Hare
3. Dogrib
4. Slave
5. Sekani
6. Beaver
7. Chipewyan
8. Cree
9. Montagnais-Naskapi

Northwest Coast
10. Tlingit
11. Haida
12. Tsimshian
13. Bella Bella
14. Bella Coola
15. Kwakiutl
16. Nootka
17. Makah
18. Quinault

Eastern Woodlands and Southeast
19. Ojibwa
20. Algonquin
21. Micmac
22. Beothuk
23. Sauk
24. Fox
25. Kickapoo
26. Potawatomi
27. Huron
28. Iroquois
29. Seneca

30. Cayuga
31. Onondaga
32. Mohawk
33. Mohican
34. Illinois
35. Miami
36. Delaware
37. Powhatan
38. Shawnee
39. Chickasaw
40. Cherokee
41. Creek
42. Natchez
43. Chocktaw

Plains
44. Sarsi
45. Blackfoot
46. Nez Perce
47. Assiniboine
48. Crow
49. Mandan
50. Yanktonai
51. Cheyenne
52. Dakota
53. Ute
54. Arapaho
55. Pawnee
56. Iowa
57. Kansa
58. Missouri
59. Kiowa
60. Osage
61. Quapaw
62. Comanche

63. Wichita
64. Lipan
65. Tonkawa

Far West
66. Yurok
67. Northern Paiute
68. Shoshone
69. Yuki
70. Wintun
71. Pomo
72. Maidu
73. Miwok
74. Mono
75. Panamint
76. Yokuts
77. Chumash
78. Cochimi

Southwest
79. Havasupai
80. Hopi
81. Mohave
82. Navajo
83. Zuni
84. Jicarilla
85. Papago
86. Apache
87. Pima
88. Chiricahua
89. Mescalero
90. Opata
91. Jumano
92. Coahuiltec

FOREWORD

The collections of North American Indian material in the Ulster Museum are extensive and of good quality. Some of the material, at least, was collected at a sufficiently early date to make it important. The fact that much of it was collected by early Ulster travellers adds a new (but only because previously unnoticed) and interesting dimension to the saga of the Irish in America. It is undoubtedly our privilege that so much of such an exciting complex of cultures should be preserved in our collections. This present book, on which Winifred Glover has worked so assiduously, was born of a small exhibition of North American Indian material displayed as part of the Ulster Museum's contribution to the Bicentenary of the United States. We feel that it was the most fitting contribution we could make.

Laurence N. W. Flanagan
Keeper of Antiquities

THE LAND OF THE BRAVE

The material in this book is all from the North American Collection in the Ulster Museum. It illustrates vividly the varied artistic achievement of many tribes and provides a valuable insight into the life style of the Native Americans who inhabited the coasts, woods and plains of the North American continent in the nineteenth and twentieth centuries.

Many of the specimens were contained in the collection of Gordon Augustus Thomson (1799-1886), born in Whitehouse, whose love of adventure started in 1826 when he was invited by an uncle to live in the West Indies. This was to be the beginning of a lifetime spent travelling the four continents collecting rare and important specimens from the native craftsmen he encountered on his journeys. He donated most of his collection to the Belfast Natural History and Philosophical Society in the years 1834 and 1843 and several pieces in later years. This collection eventually passed to the Ulster Museum. It contained many important American Indian specimens such as a rare Californian feather cloak and a splendid finger woven sash from the Woodlands area of Eastern America. From the Northwest Coast, whose craftsmen exhibited an ornate and distinctive art style most pleasing to the European eye, he also acquired a wealth of artifacts which includes one of the finest bent wood boxes produced by a Haida wood carver.

As well as the Thomson Collection, the Museum has a very fine selection of Californian-Oregon basketwork for which the native craftswomen of that area were justly famous. These baskets were gathered together by A. W. de la Cour Carroll of Ardglass who lived in America for about seventeen years. In 1898-9 he lived at Lone Pine, California and it is thought that it was during this time that most of the baskets were collected. Thanks to the generosity of his family, his entire collection illustrating good Californian types and a representative selection of baskets from several tribes outside the Californian region, was donated to the Museum in 1940 and in 1958.

Archaeological evidence has shown that the continent of North America has been colonised since prehistoric times. Alaska is divided from Siberia by the Bering Strait and it is believed that during the period from about 28,000-25,000 B.C., when there were successive advances and retreats of the polar ice, a bridge of frozen water was formed across the Bering Strait. This enabled the first wave of settlers of proto-Mongoloid stock to leave the upheaval of their native Asian homeland and make their way to their new home. The earliest accepted radio-carbon date for an artifact in North America is that of c. 20,000 B.C. obtained from a caribou shin bone scraper from the Canadian Yukon.[1]

Although colonised for thousands of years by the native Americans, it was as a result of the impact made by European traders and settlers that the Indian tribes of the eighteenth, nineteenth and twentieth centuries are best known to us and it is their artifacts that most frequently occur in museums throughout the world.

The reasons for this are both military and economic. From the fifthteenth to the eighteenth centuries, the French, English and Dutch explored and colonised the North East while the Spanish moved into the South and Southwest. It was the Spanish settlers in the Desert West who introduced the horse which was quickly adopted by the Plains Indians. The Navaho, Apache, Comanche and Ute became proficient horsemen. Large fur trading companies were established in the North by the Russians while the French and English used the Indians as scouts and mercenaries in their conflicts. The dashing horsemen of the Plains

1

provided literature and cinema with the archetypal Indian brave, a fierce warrior in feathered head-dress, hunting bison on horseback. While this is a reasonable description of the Plains Indian, it certainly does not apply to the other tribes who exhibited a wide variety of life styles and dress and formed some 650 language groups. It is only now that specimens in world-wide collections are being appreciated as a unique record illuminating a civilisation, art form and life-style which no longer exists and cannot be replaced.

The North American continent can be divided into geographical areas differing from each other in climate, animal population and vegetation. The resources of each area were exploited to the full by the tribes who settled there and their life styles were in turn affected by the resources available. Tribes occupying each area had a general similarity of dress, customs and ideas so that the term culture was applied to the conglomeration of tribes living in that area. It should always be remembered that the tribes traded with each other long before they traded with Europeans and sometimes cultural boundaries became less clearly defined. This is especially true when considering the basket making techniques of the Californian Indians. Although peace-loving, they did fight from time to time with neighbouring tribes, and womenfolk were often captured in this manner, bringing their technical skills with them and eventually adapting them to their new environment.

The Subarctic covering interior Alaska and Northern Canada to Hudson Bay had as its main tribes the Kutchin, Hare, Chipewyan and Cree. The Eastern Woodlands which extend from the Great Lakes of Canada, east to the Atlantic sea-board and south to the Gulf of Mexico, had as its principal tribes the Algonquin, Iroquois, Ojibwa, Cherokee, Chocktaw, Mohican, Delaware and Natchez. The Great Plains are the open grassland regions lying west of the Mississippi to the Rocky Mountains and north from the Gulf of Mexico into the modern Canadian provinces of Alberta and Saskatchewan. The tribes of this area are probably the most well-known; Sioux, Blackfoot, Crow, Cheyenne, Comanche, Kiowa, Pawnee and Omaha. Although only one of these tribes, the Teton Sioux, actually wore the feather war bonnet, it became the symbol of the American Indian. The Northwest Coast extends from the Pacific Coast of British Columbia and Vancouver Island south to the Columbia river. The tribes of this region were the Tlingit, Nootka, Bella Coola, Haida, Kwakiutl and Tsimshian. The Far West, which incorporates the States of California and Oregon, was the home of the Hupa, Maidu and Pomo and very many other small tribes with probably not much more than one hundred individuals in each. The final geographical area is the Southwest containing the States of Arizona and New Mexico. In this area two distinct types of civilisation co-existed, not always peaceably. The Pueblo Indians such as the Hopi, Zuni, Pima and Yuma, were sedentary farmers who lived in permanent villages. The nomadic Navajo and Apache lived in skin covered tipis; whereas the Apache used these all year round, the Navaho constructed earth covered lodges for winter living.

THE NORTHWEST COAST

The Northwest Coast tribes were famous for their ornate and distinctive art style in sculpture, painting and weaving, which reached its peak in the eighteenth and nineteenth centuries. The essential feature of their decorative art was the representation of animal forms, often very much stylised and often distorted to fit into the decorative field. Certain features of the animal, such as the dorsal fin of the killer whale, the incisor teeth of the beaver or the beak of a bird, were much emphasised and the other parts reduced in size. Birds and animals most commonly represented were the beaver, bear, wolf, hawk, eagle, raven, killer whale, seal, frog, shark and fish.[2] Their art motifs were taken from the animal life surrounding them and were a direct response to their natural environment.

The men of the tribes were excellent wood carvers and expressive representations of men and animals were carved on boxes, spear throwers, dishes and everyday articles such as spoons and pipes. The horn of mountain sheep and goats was also widely used for making spoons and dishes, especially by the Tlingit Indians. It was first boiled to soften it and then carved. Ivory, obtained from walrus tusks, seal and killer whale teeth provided another material for the Northwest Coast carvers.[3]

As well as wood and horn, a slate-like material, argillite, deposits of which are only found on the Queen Charlotte Islands, was carved into pipes, dishes, miniature totem poles and sceptres. When mined, argillite was soft and damp and it was carved in that state. After exposure to air, it dried and became hard and pipes made from this material were much valued as trade objects. Only the less ornate and more conventionally shaped pipes were used for smoking.

Articles such as shields, hats, rattles and masks for use on ceremonial occasions were often painted with mineral-based dyes to add to their artistic and dramatic appeal.

The Northwest Coast tribes had a complex social organisation formed of three distinct classes, the chiefs, middle class and slaves who most often were war captives. In the summer months family groups lived in temporary camps (on lands to which they had hereditary rights) where deer, bear and elk were hunted. In wintertime they lived in communal houses in permanent villages and huge totem poles carved with the family crests were erected in front of the houses of the Tlingit, Haida and Tsimshian chiefs.

During the winter months, feasts and ceremonies were held for both secular and religious purposes and it was during these that shields and carved wooden and copper masks would have been worn to enact dances based on ancient legend in the flickering glow of log fires. The best known of these feasts were potlatches, especially among the Kwaikiutl. At these large gatherings which were held for the public pronouncement of hereditary hunting rights, weddings and funerals, enormous quantities of goods and food were distributed to specially invited guests. They reached spectacular proportions in the nineteenth century when the traders' desire for furs and control of the great salmon fishing areas provided the tribes with tremendous wealth in a short space of time. The potlatches were often scenes of great personal rivalry among chiefs who gave away and destroyed valued articles in an attempt to outdo one another. The more one gave away or destroyed, the greater the prestige. Eventually potlatching was outlawed, but it still continued to a lesser extent.

The only musical instruments possessed by Indian tribes were whistles, rattles, flutes, drums and various types of wooden clappers. These were used to accompany the chanting voices on ceremonial occasions.

The tribes of this region were great seafarers and warriors. Fishing from large sea-going dug-outs, the Nootka hunted whales and other tribes caught sea otters, seals and many large fish with harpoons and fishing hooks. Harpoons with floats made from seal gut and detachable bone heads were one example of their extensive fishing equipment. On land they hunted deer, bear and elk with bows, arrows and lances. Strongly made composite bows, strengthened with bone and bound with gut, and arrowheads with detachable barbed bone heads are examples of their efficient hunting gear.

Although many tribes of North America were advanced in social organisation, theirs really represented the greatest achievement of Stone Age civilisation. They did make copper masks, weapons and lip ornaments but these were produced by cold hammering techniques and the technical art of metal smelting was not one which they practised. They formed stone arrows and spearheads from prehistoric times and continue the tradition to the present time. When metal tomahawks and knives came into use it was because they had been obtained as trade goods.

Their clothing was simple, consisting of woven fibre cloaks and woven hats. They went barefoot all year round since they did little land travel. Haida womenfolk were skilful weavers whose speciality was a conical spruce root hat in twined weaving which was waterproof. These were worn by fairly wealthy tribal members and the decoration was added after completion by painting designs and sewing on shells for special occasions. Sometimes the weaver incorporated European styles and produced hat styles like baker boy caps.

Tlingit women excelled in the art of basket weaving and baskets in bright colours were made in a technique known as false embroidery. Although the coloured decoration was contained in the actual weave, its appearance suggests it was added embroidery. Other smaller, less powerful Northwest Coast tribes such as the Quinault and Makah were also splendid basket weavers.

Tattooing was practised by both men and women and their love of personal adornment is further illustrated by the wearing of ear, nose and hair ornaments. On reaching puberty, girls inserted a labret in the lower lip. These were often of wood but sometimes elaborate copper ones inset with shell were worn by those who could afford them. Specially made cradles were used to flatten the heads of babies and headbinding was also employed to elongate their skulls. A normally shaped head was considered the mark of a slave:[4] Ordinary cradles were also used for babies and many attractively woven examples were produced.

Many Indian tribes loved to gamble and the Northwest Coast tribes were no exception. Gambling sticks, each painted differently, were used and one game involved guessing which ones would be visible when they were thrown in a heap.

Although the tribes of the Northwest Coast were not driven on to reservations they suffered greatly from diseases brought by the traders and from the loss of their fishing rights. In 1820 the Hudson Bay Company was formed and in 1870 the first fish canneries were established.[5] Today most of their descendants work in the salmon canneries and bitter disputes still rage over fishing rights. There has been a recent revival of stone and wood carving and painting by younger tribal artists.

SUBARCTIC

The Kutchin, Hare, Chipewyan and war-like Cree tribes based their economy on hunting caribou, moose, bear, fish and fur animals. Their weaponry consisted of bows and arrows, lances, nets, hooks and traps. The animal skins were made into shirts and trousers, often decorated with dyed bird or porcupine quills or trade beads. Quills were first chewed to soften them, coloured by boiling in vegetable-based dyes and sewn on in many patterns.[6] In 1607 the first bottle glass making house was set up in Virginia and in 1622 another house was added for the sole purpose of making glass beads for trading with the Indians, who quickly adopted them.[7] Through time these trade beads largely replaced the quillwork embroidery, although both styles continued side by side for some time. Splendid designs in quill and dyed moose hair were still being added to garments when Thomson was collecting in the area around 1830.

As well as hunting, they were fishers and gatherers

of roots, nuts and berries. Hunting bags of woven babiche, which was made from 'finely dissected tanned buckskin woven in openwork coiling without foundation',[8] with borders of deerskin, decorated with dyed quills and beads, the mesh ornamented with wool and deerskin tassels, were employed for containing their prey.

The womenfolk expressed their artistic talents in decorating bags and clothing with bird and porcupine quills while the men were proficient stone carvers, manufacturing smoking pipes and ornaments.

The tribes of this area lived in skin or bark covered conical huts and made plates and dishes from wood and birch bark. They also used birch bark for constructing canoes, while on land they had toboggans pulled by dogs, or snow shoes if travelling on foot.

Their homeland was opened up swiftly by Russian and French fur traders who exchanged European goods and clothing for pelts. The Indians readily adopted the new ideas which led to a gradual loss of their own skills. This coupled with an inability to withstand common diseases such as measles, brought by the traders, greatly depleted their numbers. A few hunters still remain today, the Cree tribe being the largest surviving.

EASTERN WOODLANDS [and South East Mound Builders]

The Iroquois League, some of whose members are those depicted in the lithograph (*frontispiece*) which was executed by Denis Dighton about 1822 when he was military painter to the Prince of Wales, had the most sophisticated form of tribal government, known as the League of Six Nations. Originally the League consisted of five Iroquoian speaking tribes, the Mohawks, Onondagos, Senecas, Oneidas and Cayugas but they were joined about 1728 by the Tuscaroras. Each tribe managed its internal affairs but matters of general importance were considered by the League which continued to be a powerful force for many years but finally collapsed through internal dispute about which side to support in the American revolution and recent attempts at revival have met with no success. It is interesting that the Seneca still regard themselves as one of the League of Six Nations and separate from the rest of the United States. Because of a land treaty entered into by their ancestors, they stand to regain the town of Salamanca in 1990 when the ninety-nine year lease to the 'white' settlers runs out.

For clothing the tribes of the Eastern Woodlands wore deerskin or bearskin robes, often painted, with low soft moccasins and kilts. The women wore deerskin wrapover skirts with poncho style tops often decorated with quilled embroidery. Huron and Iroquois women formed naturalistic floral designs in quillwork on bags and moccasins and dyed moose hair was also used as decoration. Birch bark dishes and containers were often decorated with floral designs in moose hair. The Micmac tribe of Nova Scotia specialised in making beautiful boxes with closely fitting lids from birch bark covered with brilliantly coloured quillwork in geometric designs. The menfolk of the Iroquois tribes carved wooden masks for their false face societies, a tradition which still continues.

Deer, bear and fish were hunted while maize, wild rice and tobacco were grown. As well as growing food plants such as maize, they also gathered berries, nuts and roots. Pouches and hats were often made from whole otter skins. Finely made deerskin pouches or bags with quillwork decoration demonstrate another of their food animals and a use made of the hide other than for clothing.

Wooden ball-headed clubs with a small animal carved on the top were the characteristic weapon of the Eastern Woodlands, as well as stone knives which were later replaced by iron trade knives. Bows, arrows and tomahawks, again made from trade iron, were both hunting and fighting equipment. Bark canoes, similar to the Subarctic type, and dug outs provided their water transport.

Certain tribes favoured different styles of housing; the Algonquin constructed conical huts of bark or skin called wigwams, while the Iroquois preferred long houses of bark.

It was from the Algonquian language that words were borrowed which were used to apply to all Indians, such as squaw, papoose, wigwam, moccasin, tomahawk, wampum and many others.

In prehistoric times the South East part of the Eastern Woodlands region was occupied by tribes of the most advanced material culture. They constructed enormous mounds and temples and their excavated burials have revealed the richness of their equipment.

In historic times, the Natchez, Creek, Cherokee, Chocktaw and Powhatan were the principal tribes. The Natchez, whose power was broken by the French around 1735, were the most civilised of the tribes, in European terms. They had a well-established social system and were sun worshippers. The Creeks also were a powerful tribe in the sixteenth and seventeenth centuries. By the early nineteenth century however, the Natchez and Powhatan tribe, of whom Pocahontas had been a member, had almost been destroyed by disease and the ravages of war, and the Creeks, Cherokee, Chocktaw and Chickasaw were forced from 1835-40 to move to Oklahoma. Thousands died on the forced marches but some Cherokee and Seminole, a branch of the Creeks, held out in Carolina and Florida. Today the Seminole of Florida are making strenuous efforts to revive their art forms and are on their way of becoming self-sufficient. Happily for the survivors of the Oklahoma reservations, the state turned out to be rich in oil and their descendants are reaping some benefit from what was once an alien landscape.

These tribes also hunted deer, bear, fish, grew maize and tobacco and gathered nuts, berries and shellfish. Deerskin robes and aprons often decorated with wampum (the inside of the sea clam shell, also used for currency) were worn as were bird-feather cloaks. Both face-painting and tattooing were practised by both sexes. Villages formed of mud-daubed cane huts and grass covered huts, often stockaded with wood and earthen ramparts, provided their dwellings.

The women were potters while the men were master stone carvers and native copper was worked into copper axes and ornaments by them.

THE GREAT PLAINS

The tribes of this area are probably the best known because this was the last part of America to be conquered and their long and frequently successful battles with the United States Cavalry have become part of American mythology. Among their famous chiefs were Sitting Bull, Red Cloud, Crazy Horse (Teton Sioux), Satank and Setainte (Kiowa) and Quanah Parker (Comanche).

They led a nomadic life, following the buffalo herds, living in portable skin tipis, eating the meat and clothing themselves in the skins of their quarry. Strips of meat were dried and mixed with berries to provide pemmican when fresh food was not available. When travelling they carried this in rawhide bags called parfleches.[9] For journeying across country, they used an A-shaped construction of poles, called a travois, harnessed to the horse.

The Omaha, Pawnee and Mandan used tipis only on hunting expeditions, preferring to live in earth covered lodges for the rest of the year. They grew maize at their permanent villages.

Buckskin shirts fringed with scalp locks, breech cloths, leggings and moccasins highly decorated with quills and beads in geometric patterns were worn. Body-paint and feather decorations were very popular and they painted buffalo robes and tipis to commemorate hunting and fighting exploits. Highly decorated clothing was carefully stored in special bags and kept for ceremonial occasions.

In combat they carried bows, arrows, lances, stone-headed clubs and circular painted buffalo hide shields, although these offered magical rather than physical protection to the carrier.[10] A typical example of their military equipment was an ovoid stone-headed club, bound with beads, its handle also bound with beads and horse hair.

Their horse riding skills were legendary and the Nez Perce developed a breed of horse called the Appaloosa which is still famous today.

In beadwork, many of the designs and colours were symbolic. For example, in Northern Plains Arapaho styles, small square pink spots on the body of the design indicated the bare skin on the sole of the foot; white bead work was sand or soil and blue beads often indicated water while on bags, leather fringes represented trees. Brightly woven bags with geometric decoration were made by Nez Perce women from wild hemp grass and the wool of Rocky Mountain sheep.

Plains tribes tended to keep to family hunting grounds for most of the year but came together at large tribal gatherings such as ceremonial occasions or the massed bison hunt. Male tribal members had many secret societies to which they gained admittance by a series of initiations. The spirit world was sought through visions which, like those of the early Christian ascetics, were the result of isolation, starvation and self-mutilation. Visions obtained were taken as advice from the spirit world and objects or animals seen in their trances would be depicted on shields or wearing apparel.[11]

Shamans, or medicine men, were important members of Indian society and their ability to contact the spirit world assisted them in this role. As in many societies, it was thought that sickness was caused by supernatural means and so needed supernatural remedies to effect a cure. Painted rattles formed of hide attached to a curved wooden stick and filled with small pebbles were part of the paraphernalia of the shaman.

The Teton Sioux, so-named because they inhabited the area round the Teton River, were the only tribe to wear the long flowing feather war bonnet. Among the Ulster Museum's collection is a more modest version which is made of eagle feathers set into a painted hide band with a long tail of painted hide bound at intervals with blue beads and ending with a fringe of five owl's feathers, one of which is now missing.

Their culture expanded in the eighteenth and flourished in the nineteenth centuries but when the white hunters helped to exterminate the buffalo, they were crushed and starved into submission. Since their subsistence depended so greatly on the buffalo and on being free to roam the vast plains, with their food supply gone and their lands being eaten up by the white settlers, it has been much harder for their descendants to retain their tribal origins and little trace of their former glory can be recaptured except the tributes to their passing in the museums of the world.

FAR WEST

The economy of the tribes living in the States of Oregon and California was based on seed gathering, supplemented by hunting deer and catching fish. Their clothing was made from deerskin and they lived in brush shelters or underground huts. For hunting they used bows and arrows, fish spears and traps. On land they travelled on foot and for water travel made roughly constructed dug-outs.

Although they had few material possessions, they

exhibited unsurpassed skill in basket weaving. Many different weaving styles were used and often bird feathers were woven into the pattern of baskets made by the Pomo tribe. Shells were also used as decoration and baskets ornamented in this manner were called wedding or treasure baskets. Their techniques have been classified as seven kinds of twined basketry and six kinds of coiled basketry.[12]

Nearly every tribe of North America made baskets although the Central Plains tribes relied mainly on skin containers because of the ready availability of hides. The Far Western basketmakers remain unchallenged because of their diversity and unmatched skill. This region is the most mixed of any part of America; practically every linguistic group is represented here and perhaps the availability of raw materials combined with the inter-mixture of tribes accounts for the imagination, beauty and unlimited variety of basketwork containers.

The finest textile plants for making basketry are to be found in California and in support of this statement, Mason[13] lists twenty-eight plants used by the Pomo Indians and Round Valley dwellers. They range from most kinds of sedge grasses to the stems of honeysuckle, including stems of the maidenhair fern, rootstocks of sedge and Red Bud.

The innumerable uses to which basketwork was put included the making of hats, cradles, baking baskets, acorn harvesting equipment, ladles, water jars and plates. The Paiute, who lived a nomadic existence in the desert of the Great Basin, lived in brush covered shelters and were excellent weavers. Tightly woven basketwork water carriers, pitched with pine gum are typical of their manufacture. The Shoshone had a similar way of life, were excellent basketmakers and their seasonal wandering enabled them to subsist on the wild seeds, roots and small animals provided by the land.

Although much of their time was spent in harvest-ing the resources of their environment to keep themselves alive, there was still time for recreation and ceremony. The men held ritual gatherings and both sexes loved to smoke and gamble.

One of the most colourful specimens from the Californian region is a quilled head band 1.19m. long, made from the feathers of the Northern flicker and the Red-shafted flicker (*Colaptes auratus* and *Colaptes cafer*). It illustrates how the Californian-Oregon Indians used feathers from the multitude of bird life surrounding them to enhance their basketry, to provide personal decoration and by using bird skins and feathers to make blankets, to provide extra warmth.

They were gentle seed and food gatherers and for that very reason, unable to withstand the onslaught of settlers and the rapacious gold-seeking forty-niners who used to hunt them for sport.

THE SOUTHWEST

In this area co-existed two distinct types of civilisation, the first sedentary farmers and the second the nomadic horsemen and deer hunters. The sedentary farmers were the Pueblo Indians such as the Hopi and Zuni who lived in permanent villages (pueblos) made of mud (adobe) and stone. They excelled in the arts of weaving and pottery making. They grew corn, maize, squashes and beans and held colourful dances and ceremonies which they perform to this day. The two beautifully coloured Hopi plates are typical examples of their workmanship and would have been used by the women of the tribe in their dances.

The Pima and Yuma also grew corn but did not hold the Pueblo ceremonies. They lived in round mud and log huts and travelled on foot, only very occasionally using horses. They too were excellent weavers and made enormous coiled baskets for food storage.

The Pueblos wove fine cotton which they used for

making brilliantly coloured clothes. The cotton was native to the area and was grown before the Spaniards introduced sheep in the sixteenth century. The weaving was done by the menfolk while the womenfolk of the Hopi and Zuni and San Ildefonso were famous for pottery making.

All the natives of the Southwest excelled in the art of basket making. The Hopi, Pima and Papago were well known for their coiled basketwork and the Oraibi specialised in flat wicker baskets. The Apache produced a very wide range of well made containers, using the coil method, including pitch-covered watertight jars and huge storage and burden baskets.

The nomadic Navajo and Apache lived in skin-covered tipis and whereas the Apache used these all year round, the Navajo constructed earth covered lodges, called hogans, for winter living. Both tribes made undecorated pottery for everyday use.

The Navajo specialised in the art of weaving. They produced, on their primitive looms, beautiful blankets from sheep's wool, brilliantly coloured with vegetable dyes. Many of their designs were significant, for example a chief's blanket had horizontal stripes, a central design and repeats of part of the design in each corner. From 1853 onwards, the Navajo developed into fine silversmiths, an art they had learned from the Mexicans.

Today the Pueblo Indians still retain their traditional skills and ceremonials. The Navajo are successful sheep farmers and silversmiths and number 140,000, the largest surviving of the Indian tribes.

The Apache who are the best known of the tribes, chiefly because of their fighting skill, and whose chiefs such as Geronimo, Mangas Colorado, Vittorio and Cochise became famous for their lightning raids, were almost wiped out. The Mescalero Apache are recovering and becoming cattle farmers.

From the illustrated examples of the North American material in the Ulster Museum it can be seen that the civilisation of the native population was very broadly based indeed, incorporating the artistic force of the Northwest Coast tribes, the political skill of the Iroquois nation and the technical excellence of the peaceful tribes of California. The least tribute that Museums possessing examples of their art and artifacts can pay to the tribes, some of whom have managed to survive in name only, is to display to the rest of the world and their descendants, the wealth of their achievements.

ANDREW WILLIAM DE LA COUR CARROLL [1845-1920]

A. W. de la Cour Carroll was born at Ardglass, Co. Down in the year 1845. His father was Andrew de la Cour Carroll, a Commander in the Royal Navy and his mother Mary Hutchinson Carroll. Four boys and one girl were born but one son died in infancy and another brother, who was the only son to follow his father's profession, died on board HMS *Galatea* at Halifax, Nova Scotia in 1865 at the age of eighteen.

Throughout his life A. W. de la Cour Carroll was close to his younger brother Robert Henry Wright Carroll who was friendly and outgoing in marked contrast to his own shy and retiring personality. Robert bequeathed Andrew's basketry collection to the Museum in his own will of 1940 with the provision that it should be known thereafter as the Andrew W. de la Cour Carroll Collection.

Apart from their Navy connections, his family owned property, including a well established public house at Howth, Co. Dublin and Andrew W. de la Cour Carroll had substantial business interests in the timber trade, one of the reasons, it is supposed, he spent almost seventeen years in America.

Throughout his life, 'Willie', as he was known to his friends, was a quiet, unassuming man who did not marry and had a strong interest in the Church of Ireland, being listed as a registered Vestryman from 1879-1883, the year he left for America. He returned to Ireland about 1900 as his name again appears as a Vestry man in the Church registers and he continued his Church interests up to the time of his death in 1920.

Of medium height and squarely built he was athletic in his youth and long jumped a distance of twenty-two feet on the village green. This was a considerable feat and it is believed, a record for the day.

In 1898-9 he was living at Lone Pine, California and it is probable that it was during this time that he collected most of the baskets. He corresponded with O. T. Mason, of the Smithsonian Institution, New York who was a noted scholar of the North American Indian. In Volume II of his book, *Indian Basketry*, Mason listed Carroll among the collectors describing his basket-work as, 'good Californian types'.

When he returned to Ireland about 1900, his disposition, which had always been shy and retiring, became more so with the passing years and towards his death he was virtually a recluse in Burford Lodge, Ardglass. He was buried at Ardglass graveyard in 1920 in the family grave.

It is fortunate that thanks to the generosity of his family his fine collection remains a tribute to his memory and to the skill and excellence of the Californian basketmakers of the nineteenth century.

GORDON AUGUSTUS THOMSON [1799-1886]

G. A. Thomson, the son of John Thomson of Jennymount, Whitehouse (later re-named Castleton), was born on 21 September 1799 into a wealthy and strongly Presbyterian family. Early in his adventurous life he acquired the nickname 'Galloper' given to him on the occasion of a ride from Belfast to Dublin for a wager which he won and throughout his life he kept his nickname as well as his love of horses. He married in his twenty-fifth year and two daughters were born, Mattie and Margaret.

In 1826 he set sail for St. Vincent in the West Indies where his Mother's Uncle, Colonel Gordon, had a sugar plantation. This was to be the start of a life spent travelling the four continents and, being fortunate enough to be possessed of substantial private means and a yacht, he was able to gratify his life-long passion.

In 1831 he joined the ship HMS *Pelorus* which was on a mission to African waters in pursuit of slave ships. He participated in the capture of a large slaver at

Sierra Leone and the book *Men of the Time in Australia*[14] notes that he was appalled at the conditions on board. From Sierra Leone, the *Pelorus* set sail for Benin, again in quest of slavers. On this occasion the ship almost came into conflict with another British man-of-war, both vessels thinking the other was their enemy.

The Cape of Good Hope was his next port of call and disembarking there he spent the next six months exploring the African continent where he again acquired several pieces of ethnographic interest. On completion of this part of his quest, he set sail for St. Helena, Bombay and China where he was the guest in Canton of Thomas Dent, an important merchant.

Restless again, he departed for Melbourne in 1834 where he camped among the small group of mud huts which was the foundation of what was to be the powerful city we know today. He was fond in later life of claiming that he was Melbourne's oldest inhabitant and it is very likely to have been true. In *Fragments that Remain*[15] is mentioned the fact that he collected many aboriginal weapons from the native population but he did not donate these to the Belfast Natural History and Philosophical Society.

Around 1835 he arrived in Sydney for a short stay and soon departed for Tasmania. His next target was New Zealand and a cruise of the South Sea Islands. It was during this time that he bought the well known Hawaiian feather cloak which King Kamehameha III was selling, among other valuable items, to pay off an indemnity to the French, for injuries received. He visited Tahiti before it came under French rule, where he met Queen Pomare and it is probable that what is known as the Tapa cloth cloak worn by a lady of the Royal Family belonged to her.

He travelled from Tahiti via whaler to Valparaiso where he was appointed King's Messenger by Admiral Sir Graham Hammond, Naval Commander of the South American Station. His mission was to carry despatches across the Pampas and the Andes and in 1838 he made the marathon ride from Rio to Valparaiso in eight days, a record for the time. From South America he travelled to Cuba, Jamaica, the United States and Canada, collecting on the way. It is likely that he visited North America twice as he donated North American specimens to the Belfast Natural History and Philosophical Society both in 1834 and in 1843.

He still retained a deep fondness for the country of his birth and in 1850 he returned to spend a year living with his brother Robert at Castleton, the family seat, while he had his home, Bedeque House, built on the Crumlin Road on what is now the site of the Mater Hospital. This was to be his base more or less permanently for the next nineteen years but his wanderlust exerted itself from time to time and in 1867 he voyaged to Egypt and Palestine.

Finally he set out on his last journey to Melbourne in 1872. There he built another home, again called Bedeque House and became a grand old man of the city. He wrote a short account of his travels for the Melbourne newspaper *Argus* and it is a mark of the eminence to which he rose in Melbourne society that on his death in 1886 the *Argus* devoted a double column to his obituary.

Throughout his eventful life he was charitable and philanthropic and it is most fortunate for posterity that with his insatiable appetite for the curious and unusual he punctuated his travels by acquiring, from wherever he visited, what have now become very important ethnographic specimens from many races extinguished by the advance of civilisation.

CATALOGUE

The catalogue is in two sections, the first containing those items which are illustrated, grouped in regions: Northwest Coast; Subarctic; Eastern Woodlands; Plains; the Far West; the Southwest. The second part, containing the unillustrated material, is grouped functionally; Footwear; Headgear; Ornaments; Other Clothing; Cradles; Models; Boxes; Bags; Basketry; Pottery; Amusements; Tools; Weapons and Miscellaneous.

Section I:
Illustrated Specimens

The Northwest Coast

1. BOW (1.29m.) and **ARROW** (92cm.)
Shaped composite bow of wood strengthened with twisted gut and strip of bone. The bowstring is of twisted fibre.[16] The arrow is of wood with a detachable four-barbed head made of bone and three-feathered nock.
Thomson Coll. 1910:736

2. LIDDED CONTAINER (14.6cm. diam.)
Circular lidded container in wrapped twined weaving. The base and rim are brown, the body and lid cream coloured, decorated with red pendant triangles, the intervening spaces filled with yellow and bordered by a purple line.
Makah Indian, Washington.
de la Cour Carroll Coll. LCC 35

3. TRINKET BASKET (10cm. wide, 7cm. hgt.)
Small oblong container in fine twined weaving in cream with two horizontal rows of brown, yellow and red stripes beneath shoulder and just above base. The middle zone and the lid top have a running chevron in brown.
Makah Indian, Washington.
de la Cour Carroll Coll. LCC 44

4. LIDDED BASKET (15cm. diam.)
Lidded basket with rim strengthened by a wooden splint. Design of three canoes woven in purple in false embroidery and a further band of false embroidery in white and purple near base.
Quinault Indian.
de la Cour Carroll Coll. 21:1946

5. CRADLE (65cm.)
Strongly-made boat-shaped carrying cradle in imbricated basketwork. The sides are decorated with black and cream and red dyed cane and the carrying straps of leather are fastened to the sides in four places.
Thomson-Frazer River tribes.
A. MacDonald. 1939:274

6. GAMBLING STICKS
a. Set of twenty-one gambling sticks from the North-west Coast, each one marked differently with painted bands.
Thomson Coll. 1916:32

b. Set of four gambling sticks (34cm.) used by female members of the Pomo tribe. They are of natural wood and have lozenge decoration burned into the curved side.
de la Cour Carroll Coll. LCC 55

The Pomo game involved throwing the sticks to the ground and points were awarded according to which side turned up. Two or four persons could play, the first person obtaining twelve points being the winner. Most tribes loved to gamble and for this purpose used painted sticks and also basketwork gambling trays with dice. The dice of the Far West tribes were usually made of gum-filled, shell-inlaid pine nut shells.

7. HARPOON (17cm.) and **SHEATH**
Ground slate harpoon head in barbed bone holder. The wooden sheath is bound with gut. This specimen is much older than the nineteenth century as very similar articles to this were being made when Cook brought back examples from his third voyage.

Probably made by Nootka of Vancouver Island.
Thomson Coll. 1910:644

8. HALIBUT HOOKS (35cm.)
a. and b. Wooden hooks with fibre bound hook with iron barb. One is carved in the shape of a squid with two bird's heads inset, the other is carved in the shape of a sculpin.
Thomson Coll. 1911:1174

9. FRONTLET (22cm. hgt. 29cm. wdth.) (colour plate I)
Wooden frontlet of hawk gripping the head of a beaver. There are holes along the top for feathers, now missing. The two portions at the side are of leather. It is made all in one piece except for the claws which are of separate plugs of wood. One has been loose and has been wedged in with a piece of gut. It is inset with abalone shell, some of which is missing. The hawk is pale blue with red lips and black eyebrows while the beaver is green with red lips and black eyebrows.
Probably Tsimshian tribe.
Thomson Coll. 1910:60

10. MASK (25cm.) (colour plate II)
Painted wooden mask in blue and black with red lips, nostrils and chequered red ears. Masks such as these were worn by secret dancing societies at which the male dancer acted the hero of legends. The ends of the fibre mouthpiece can just be seen under the nostrils.
Probably Tsimshian tribe.
Londonderry Corporation. 103:1952
See: *Illustrated Souvenir of Museum and Art Gallery,* Stranmillis, April 1954, pl. XXIIa.

11. DAGGER (57cm.)
Double-bladed copper fighting dagger with grip in centre bound with leather. Leather sheath and sling belt.

The label states 'made by Indians from local copper'.
Thomson Coll. 1910:522

12. SPRUCE ROOT HAT (41cm. diam.)
Hat made from twined spruce root and painted with totemic bird and eye decoration in red, black and blue. An interior woven band fits the wearer's head and the inside of the crown is strengthened with a circle of wood sewn on.
Haida.
Thomson Coll. 1910:264

13. SPRUCE ROOT HAT (27cm. diam)
Twined spruce root hat showing European style influence. The Indian tribes were quick to imitate European styles which resulted in the woven cap illustrated.
Possibly Haida.
Thomson Coll. 1910:266

14. GREASE DISH (20.5cm.)
Square kerfed cedar wood box in shape of beaver holding a stick in his paws. The inlay round the rim and the beaver's teeth have been created by using nut kernels. This grease dish would have been used at feasts for holding grease or oil. The most common oil was that obtained from the eulachon or candle fish. It was produced by letting the fish rot in pits for eight to fourteen days, heating but not boiling it in water and then skimming the oil off the top. It was then left to cool, re-heated to a liquid state and strained. It was considered a delicious condiment and was also nutritious since it was rich in vitamin D, and is still manufactured today.[17]
Thomson Coll. 1910:65

15. FOOD DISH (17.5cm.)
Oval dish of wood in form of beaver holding a stick between his incisor teeth and front paws.
Thomson Coll. 1910:67

16. HORN DISH (27cm.)
Dish in form of hollowed-out water bird with incised ornament on inside rim. Probably much earlier in date than 1830 since the modelling of the bird is early and there is much wear on the sides of the dish.
Thomson Coll. 1910:100

17. BOX (30cm.) (colour plate III)
Square kerfed, bent wood box with deep relief carving of hawk's heads at either end, its wings emerging from the sides. Cowrie shell inset round the rim.
Haida.
Thomson Coll. 1910:66

18. LEGGINGS (42cm. wide)
One of pair of cream-coloured dressed leather leggings with black and red painted decoration, which includes a bear's head and 'eye' motif. The tops are folded over and both they and the bottom edge are fringed. Probably worn on ceremonial occasions.
Tlingit.
Thomson Coll. 1910:231

19. RATTLE (28cm.)
Painted wooden rattle depicting kingfisher, shaman and the mythical thunderbird which was supposed to cause thunder and lightning. Rattles such as this would have been used on ceremonial occasions. Probably mid-eighteenth century in date.
Haida.
Thomson Coll. 1910:3

20. SHIELD (39cm. diam.)
Painted wooden shield with wooden strip carrying handle. Remains of hair tufts round edge. The decoration consists of black 'eye' motifs and orange claws on a green background. The animal represented may be a wolf. Probably used as a dance shield as it is only

about 2cm. thick.
Kwakiutl.
Thomson Coll. 1910:735

21. NEEDLE CASES (11.5cm. 14cm.)
Bone tubes with incised totemic decoration. The bases are filled in with pieces of wood and each has leather carrying ties.
Thomson Coll. 1925:2

22. EAR ORNAMENTS (10cm.)
Very fine ear ornaments, made from the wing bone of a large bird. They have incised black geometric decoration and are further ornamented with a string of red and white beads and black feathers.
Probably Hupa tribe, California.
Thomson Coll. 1910:326

23. HAIR ORNAMENT (11cm.)
Ornament of blue beads and dentalium shell on leather backing with leather tie. Worn by the womenfolk of the North West Coast.
Thomson Coll. 1910:321

24 SPOONS (18.5cm. and 25cm.)
Two horn spoons, each with carved handles. The larger has an unfinished grotesque human figure and animal decoration while the smaller has a handle formed of a sea monster with shell inlaid eyes and a row of shell inlay down the centre of the bowl.
Thomson Coll. 1910:111 and 112

25. SPEAR THROWER (35cm.)
Carved wooden spear thrower with eye decoration and a sea monster with protruding tongue. The atlatl or spear thrower was in use in North America from prehistoric times before the introduction of the bow and arrow.
Thomson Coll. 1910:735

26. PIPE (11.5cm.)
Argillite pipe carved with elaborately intertwined composition of birds and men. The predominant bird is the raven whose own head has a stylised human head inset. This part forms the bowl while the mouthpiece is a stylised human figure clutched by a bird. Haida.
Londonderry Corporation. 104:1952

The designs for these pipes were often based on legends and their significance has been lost through time. Sometimes a carver would create a design whose purpose would be known only to himself. Every Indian tribe smoked tobacco and pipes were made from wood, steatite, argillite and catlinite which was a reddish coloured slate.

27. PIPE (29.5cm.)
Argillite pipe depicting two men, the waves of the sea and ropes. It is meant to represent European sailors who must have been a common sight to the Haida Indians of the nineteenth century.
Thomson Coll. 1910:161

28. RATTLE BASKET (15.5cm. diam.)
Brightly coloured twined spruce-root basket with symbols in false embroidery. This covered example has small stones contained in its hollow handle to provide a pleasing sound when used.
Tlingit tribe.
Donation Mrs. M. Gordon. C40:1977

29. HARPOON (1.23m.)
Fishing spear or harpoon with wooden shaft and bone socket at one end. The head is five barbed and attached by a long cord to the shaft. A seal-gut bladder to act as a float is attached to the shaft (not shown).
Thomson Coll. 1910:716

30. WALRUS IVORY ORNAMENT (25cm.)
Ivory ornament composed of a row of small fish with the head and tail of a whale linked to each end. Two large seals hang down in the middle. Details are incised in black and the opercula of shells have been inserted for eye and tail decoration. This may have been used to embellish the clothing of a shaman.
Nootka Sound, Vancouver Island.
Thomson Coll. 1910:339

This ornament is almost certainly of Alaskan Eskimo manufacture but it is included here as there is no doubt where it was collected.[18]

Subarctic

31. SHIRT
Shirt of soft deerskin decorated with a band of woven quill ribbon of orange and white round the shoulders, each strand of the fringe bound with quill, threaded through a dried nut kernel and tipped with orange dye.
Thomson Coll. 1910:204

32. JACKET
Skin jacket with attached mittens, bordered with interlaced bands of coloured leather strips and edged with blue, white and black beads.
101:1917

33. HUNTING BAG (48cm. wide)
Bag of woven babiche with deerskin border, decorated with dyed quills and beads, the mesh ornamented with wool and deerskin tassels.
Made by Indians of Fort Good Hope, Mackenzie River, 1898.
Donation Rev. A. S. Woodward. C41:1977

34. BAG (28cm.)

Oval black cloth bag, trimmed with navy and beautifully decorated in ornate floral patterns with white, blue, pink, green and transparent beads. A small beaded handle of red and white beads is attached to the top.
Fort Good Hope, Mackenzie River, 1898.
Donation Rev. A. S. Woodward. C42:1977

35. POUCH (101cm.)

Pouch made from whole otter skin, its neck and paws bound with orange, white and blue woven quill ribbon while orange and blue moose hair tassels bound with metal trade jingles adorn its back.
Thomson Coll. 1910:289

Eastern Woodlands

36. UNFINISHED MITTEN (19.5cm.) (colour plate IV)

Unfinished mitten of black-dyed deerskin showing moose hair embroidery of the finest quality in ornate floral designs on the back, front and thumb. Possibly made as a trade object.
Huron Indian.
Thomson Coll. 1910:291

37. BIRCH BARK BOXES (22 x 18 x 16cm., 15 x 13 x 10.5cm.) (colour plate V)

Two rectangular birch bark boxes with closely fitting lids, one flat, the other domed. Both are richly ornamented with coloured quill embroidery in geometric designs.
Micmac tribe, mid-nineteenth century.
Grainger Coll. 1252 and 1254

38. PIPE (25cm.)

Tobacco pipe with stone head carved with a bear, beaver and otter holding up the bowl. The wooden stem is bound with blue and green beads.
Micmac tribe of St. John's, New Brunswick.
Donation Rev. R. Irvine, 1859. 1910:153

39. MOCCASINS (24cm. long)

Deerskin moccasins decorated with dyed moose hair tufting on instep and around heel. The instep pattern is bordered by a band of pink, white and purple quill embroidery. Probably early twentieth century.
Donation H. Conn C43:1977

40. MOCCASINS (24cm. long)

Deerskin moccasins with floral appliqué beadwork in red, green, orange, light and dark blue, bound with maroon and purple silk. Probably early twentieth century.   Donation H. Conn C28:1977

41. DISH (15cm. diam.)

Delicate octagonal dish made of birch bark panels sewn together and embroidered with moose hair in floral designs of violet and white.
Micmac
Nevin Bequest 1920:297

42. PIPE BAG (90cm.)

Long soft leather deerskin bag with scalloped top trimmed with blue beads and with floral beaded panels in overlay beadwork of different design on either side. The long fringe is threaded with blue, white and metal beads. Late nineteenth century.
C44:1977

43. POUCH (26cm.) (colour plate VI)

Deerskin pouch beautifully ornamented with orange and cream quill embroidery. The strands of the fringe are bound with orange quill.   Grainger Coll. 1253

44. CLUB (66cm.)
Characteristic Woodlands weapon of ball-headed wooden club, the head surmounted by a carved animal, in this case a snake.
W. G. Byron.
640:1954

45. POUCH (25cm.) (colour plate VII)
Black cloth envelope style bag, bordered with green silk and richly embroidered in blue, white and green beads in ornate floral and scroll patterns. Woollen tassels hang from the bottom edge and the interior is lined with pinkish floral cotton.
Said to have been made for Tuskina, Chief of the Creek Indians, by his daughter.
Donated to B.N.H. & P.S. by Mr. J. Hagan of New Orleans in 1835.
1910:271

46. BIRCH BARK CONTAINER (22cm.)
Cylindrical bark container with stamped decoration, the top and bottom made from wooden roundels. Late nineteenth century.
Canon Grainger Coll. 1297

47. CIGAR OR TOBACCO BOX (10cm.)
Small rectangular birch bark container with sleeve lid. The borders are of lengths of white ash splints. The scenes on either side in moose hair embroidery depict seated and standing Indians smoking and one panel contains a bird perched on a bush. Contains a small roll of birch bark.
Woodlands.
94:1962

Although such objects were produced for trading, the quality of workmanship is very high and illustrates the ingenuity in achieving a different product from traditional materials.

48. SASH (3m.)
Finger woven sash of wool. Such sashes were used for carrying small objects (see those depicted in the **Dighton** lithograph, frontispiece). This example of perhaps Shawnee workmanship is a very fine specimen.
Thomson Coll. 1910:232

49. MODEL CANOE (40cm.)
Canoe of wood and birch bark with quill embroidery. Birch bark canoes were constructed by sticking large strips of bark to wooden strakes. Canoes of this type were made by both the Subarctic and Woodlands tribes.
Micmac, late nineteenth century.
Nevin Bequest. 279:1920

50. LITHOGRAPH (57cm. x 43cm.) (frontispiece)
This hand-painted lithograph is the work of Deñis Dighton (1792-1827) who was appointed military draughtsman to the Prince of Wales in 1815 and made occasional trips abroad for his royal patron. In 1821 several lithographs, of which this is one, were published. The Woodlands Indians featured (probably Iroquois) of that time practised face painting (an ancient art of the region), wore ear-rings and nose ornaments and had tomahawks and pipes combined. Tomahawks and guns were introduced to the native population by the French and English in the nineteenth century. Under each figure is the name with an English version beside it. From left to right the names read: Ne-gun-ne-au-goh (Beaver); Se-gous-ken-ace (I like her); Teki-cue-doga (Two Guns); Sta-cute (Steep Rock); Uc-tau-goh (Black Squirrel); Senung-gis (Long Horns, the Chief); Ne-gui-e-et-twafaaue (Little Bear).
Purchase. C45:1977

Plains

51. HEADDRESS (lgth. of tail 58cm.)
Headdress of eagle feathers, slotted into cloth-trimmed dressed brown leather band with painted decoration in red and white, now faded. A long tail of dressed hide, originally coloured red, and bound at intervals with blue beads and leather fringes tipped with owl feathers, hangs from the back.
C46:1977

52. BEADED CUFF (19cm. deep)
One of a pair of beaded cuffs on a cloth backing, fringed with buckskin. The horizontal bands of red, white, blue and yellow beads end with a stepped diamond-shaped border in blue, green and orange with a pink centre.
Donation H. Conn. C47:1977

53. CLUB (13.5cm. head lgth.)
Spindle-shaped stone-headed club, bound with leather decorated with red and blue beads. The wooden handle (now broken) is bound with red and blue beads and black and white horsehair.
Possibly Sioux.
C48:1977

54. RATTLE (35cm.)
Hide rattle attached to a curved wooden stick and filled with small pebbles. The painted decoration is in white and red.
C49:1977

55. BAG (31 cm.)
Food gathering bag woven from wool and wild hemp grass in bright geometric patterns. The decoration consists of a rectangular panel with triangles in blue along the top and bottom. This contains four pink rectangles each containing a blue cross. The background is green

while the exact centre of the bag is marked with a yellow cross which has a red axis.
Nez Perce tribe.
C50:1977

56. SINGLE MOCCASINS (24cm. foot lgth.)
Very fine dressed leather moccasins beautifully embroidered with red and white coloured quills in geometric leaf pattern, their edges bound with purple silk. Although not a pair, they are very similar.
Donation Col. Crawford. 1910:197 and 1910:198

The Far West

57. GAMBLING TRAY (47cm.)
Fine coil weave gambling tray with band of stepped decoration in brown round edge and further three bands of running chevron decoration in black.
Coso Valley.
de la Cour Carroll Coll. LCC 31

58. TREASURE BASKET (23cm. diam.)
Beautifully made coil woven basket with stepped lightning pattern in black and black lozenges converging towards the base. Small groups of shell money are added round the rim. One orange bead still remains and traces of feathers are still visible.
Thomson Coll. 1910:143

The Pomo tribe of California took special pride in producing very high quality baskets, richly decorated with feathers, shell money and beads. These were commonly called wedding or treasure baskets.

59. CARRYING BASKET (38cm. diam.)
Conical carrying basket in plain twined weaving. The border is strengthened by a hoop of wood. Baskets

such as this were used by the Pomo Indians in harvesting acorns which largely formed their staple diet. They were carried by means of a band round the forehead and round the basket.
Donation Mrs. M. Gordon. C51:1977

60. LADLE DIPPER (22cm.)
Oval ladle or dipper with hollow handle or spout in plain twined weaving so closely worked that it is watertight.
Possibly Pomo Indian.
de la Cour Carroll Coll. 64:1946

61. CRADLEBOARD (52cm.)
The sun visor is of coarse openwork weave, the board is formed of long splints attached to shorter horizontal rods by means of tartan cloth strips in diamond-shaped woven patterns. Quite small, the label says this example was made for a girl.
Yokut tribe.
de la Cour Carroll Coll. LCC 32

62. CRADLEBOARD (84cm.)
Strongly-made baby carrier. The frame is made from a Y-shaped branch and strengthened by cross-tied wooden splints, all dyed red. The webbing is made from reed-like grass, tied at top and bottom. The babies were secured on these carrying frames by means of cloth or skin bindings and the pointed end was designed to stick into the ground so that the child could be propped up in its cradle close to where its mother was working.
Yokut tribe.
de la Cour Carroll Coll. 62:1946

63. WATER CARRIER (18cm. hgt.)
Water bottle in close twined weaving pitched with pine gum. It has two loop handles of human hair.
Paiute.   de la Cour Carroll Coll. LCC 33

64. STORAGE BASKET (24cm. hgt.)
Beautifully woven globular storage basket with cover. Arrow and diamond-shaped motifs have been woven in red wool.
Walker Lake Indians, probably Paiute, Nevada.
de la Cour Carroll Coll. LCC 34

65. HAT (21cm. diam.)
Strongly-made coil weave hat with decoration consisting of five vertical panels of black, containing inverted reddish brown arrowheads, interspersed with two opposing arrowheads between the panels.
Shoshone Indian.
de la Cour Carroll Coll. 5:1946

66. HAT (20cm. diam.)
Coil weave hat in three step pattern units of reddish brown and black from rim to crown. One stepped lightning pattern in brown. Made by Indian tribe living round Darwin, probably Paiute.
de la Cour Carroll Coll. LCC 36

67. BEAN POT (19cm. diam.)
Fine coil weave bean pot in natural colour with reddish brown and black step and lightning pattern. Black chevron design round rim.
Made by natives at Darwin, California.
de la Cour Carroll Coll. 29:1946

68. HAT (19cm. diam.)
Coil woven hat with five zones of stepped lightning pattern in brown and black. The weave incorporates white bird quills, and it illustrates how the basket maker would produce a pleasing effect despite a mistake. In one panel there are two little men and in between, two feet and legs which had to be abandoned since the completed man would have merged with the stepped lightning pattern. Darwin Indian, probably Paiute. de la Cour Carroll Coll. LCC 37

69.   SEED SIFTER (31cm.)
Elegant shield-shaped seed or acorn sifter in twined openwork weave, the perimeter rimmed with a slender twig.
Possibly Pomo Indian.
de la Cour Carroll Coll. 52:1946

70.   SEED SIFTER (52cm.)
Large and beautifully woven seed sifter of scoop shape with one zone of brown lattice decoration and one band of alternate brown and self-coloured stitches. This type of weaving is called rod-and-welt foundation by Mason and is another variety of coiled basketry.
'Bought at Eno's Camp'.
de la Cour Carroll Coll. 53:1946

71.   SEED SIFTER (25cm.)
Oval seed sifter of coarse open twined weaving made from two different coloured grass roots. The weft strands are natural coloured while the warp strands are brown, giving a pleasing mixed effect.
California.
de la Cour Carroll Coll. 51:1946

72.   QUILL HEAD BAND (1.19m.)
Head band made from the tail feathers of the red tailed and yellow tailed flickers. The tips point in both directions and are held together by two strings passed through the centre of the band. The predominant colours are light orange and black from the red-shafted flicker but several sets of yellow feathers from the Northern flicker have been set among them. Illustrated with the band is a Northern flicker to show how many of these birds would have been needed to make such a band. A little string of red and blue beads is attached to one end for fastening. Such head bands were worn by many Californian tribes; this example is very similar to those worn by the Koso or Panamint tribe.   C54:1977

73.   TWO HATS (16cm., 17cm. diam.)
a. Beautiful cream and tan hat in fine twined weaving. Star decoration on top.
Arcata, Humbolt Bay.
de la Cour Carroll Coll. LCC 38·

b. Very fine coil woven basketwork hat in cream with three zones of stepped pattern bounded on either side by a row of triangles in brown. Its label says 'bought from Geronimo's people' who were the Chiricahua Apache of the Southwest but this is not Apache work-manship. Its design is typical of Yokut weaving.
de la Cour Carroll Coll. LCC 39

74.   BOTTLENECK BASKET (10.5cm. hgt.)
Fine coil woven bottleneck basket with rattlesnake pattern in brown and black on cream. Label says 'Got from Charlie Hacket's wife, Mother Piute, Father Mono'.
de la Cour Carroll Coll. LCC 40

75.   FEATHER CLOAK (1.19m. x 1.60m.)
Cloak made of knotted string around which feathers have been wound. A band of brownish-black feathers, interspersed with several greenish feathers, is at the top and bottom edge, followed by a band of white feathers while the central portion is of mottled brown and white feathers.
California.
Thomson Coll. 1910:188

Kroeber in *Handbook of the Indians of California* says that the Maidu and Wintun tribes used to make fea-ther cloaks by either knotting feathers into woven string or by winding strips of bird skin round string. Other tribes of the Sacramento Valley also used to make and wear feather cloaks and he mentions that there were at least three techniques used in their manufacture.

The Southwest

76. SACRED PLAQUES (26cm. diam.) (colour plate VIII)
Two Hopi sacred coiled plaques in close wickerwork weave which were carried by Hopi womenfolk in their dances. The colours of red, blue, yellow, purple and black were obtained from vegetable dyes and the blue dye is said to have been manufactured from beans which they also grew as a food plant. Figure representations on these plaques were highly schematised.
de la Cour Carroll Coll. LCC 41

77. SACRED PLAQUE (37cm. diam.) (colour plate VIII)
Sacred wicker plaque from the Hopi town of Oraibi whose weavers specialised in making wicker plates. The coloured design is a spider web pattern and the whole basket is made from the root of sedge (saw grass), brilliantly coloured in orange, green, purple and brown.
de la Cour Carroll Coll. 57:1946

78. FOOD BASKET (48cm. diam.)
Enormous coiled basket for food storage. The foundation for this basket is made of grass stems and the sewing is done with splints of cottonwood or willow. The black labryinth design is done by working in martynia.
Pima Indian.
de la Cour Carroll Coll. LCC 42

79. BLANKET (1.92cm. x 1.20m.)
Heavy blanket woven in vertical stripes of black and dark blue with rectangular central portion of red, white and brown, the immediate centre being formed of a red oblong containing vertical brown and white stripes. This example is probably of fairly recent manufacture but blankets such as these were originally called chief's blankets although anyone of sufficient wealth could own one.
Navajo Indian.
Donation Mrs. Ayon. 306:1936

80. BEADED BOOTS (39cm.)
Boots of hide and dressed leather ornamented with black, red, blue and white beads. The soles are of rawhide and they have drawstring tops.
Grainger Coll. 3431

81. POUCH (30cm.)
Leather pouch decorated with blue, black, red and white beads with panels of red and white quill decoration at the top. Leather loop handle.
Grainger Coll. 3404

Both this and no. **80** come from the late nineteenth century collection of Canon Grainger and as the decoration on boots and pouch is so similar, it is possible that they represent the work of the same tribe, either Navaho or Apache.

82 DOLLS (16.5cm.) (colour plate IX)
Low-fired clay dolls, one male, one female, the male with red wool loin cloth, the female with red cotton skirt and blue and white ear-rings. Tufts of white down have been stuck on as hair. Clay dolls were made from prehistoric times throughout the Southwest. The painted decoration represents body tattooing which was once popular in this region. The bead and cloth costume were acquired from trading.
Mohave Indian, although almost identical figurines were made by the neighbouring Yuma tribe. c.1900 in date.
C43:1977

1. Bow and arrow

2. Lidded container   3. Trinket basket   4. Lidded basket

23

5. Cradle

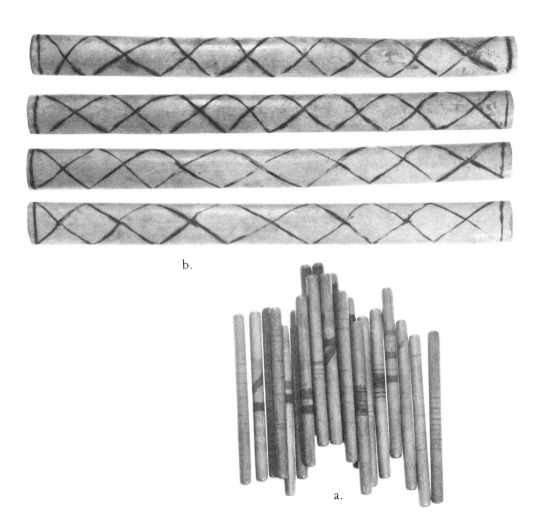

b.

a.

6.   Gambling sticks

7. Harpoon and sheath

Plate I Frontlet (cat. no. 9)

Plate II Mask (cat. no. 10)

Plate III Box (cat. no. 17)

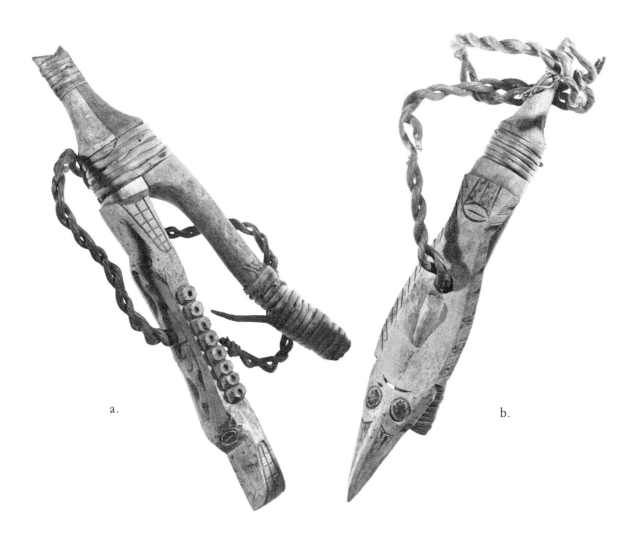

a.

b.

8.   Halibut hooks

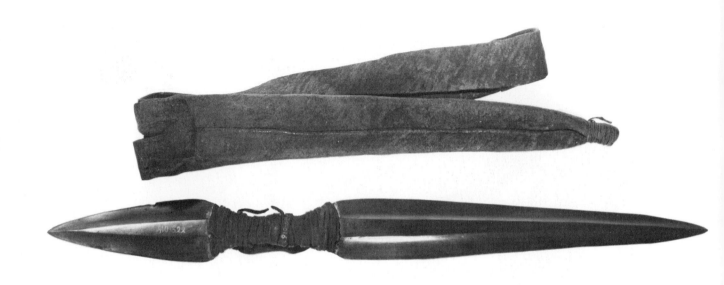

11. Dagger

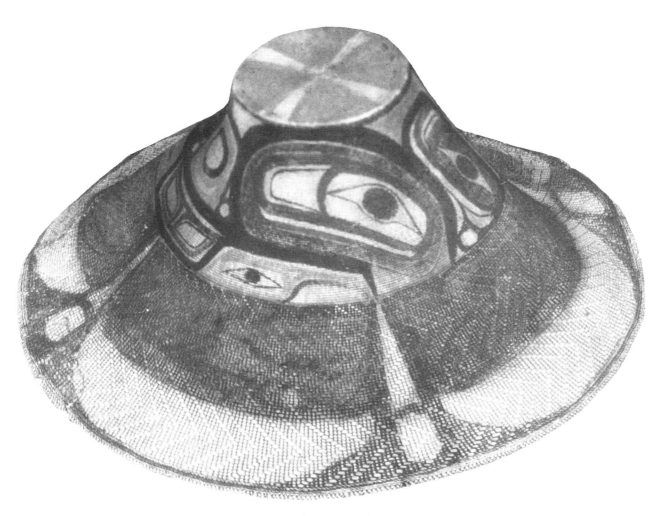

12.   Spruce root hat

13.   Spruce root hat

14.   Grease dish

15.   Food dish

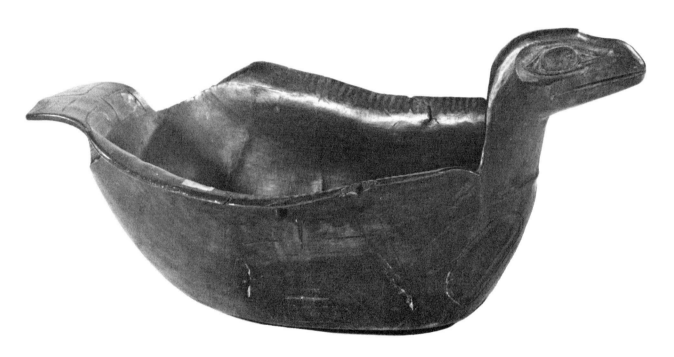

16. Horn dish

18.   Legging

19. Rattle

20. Shield

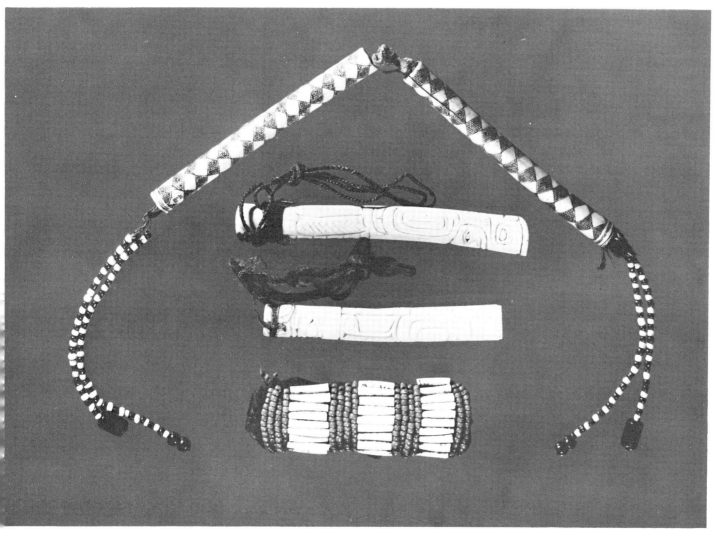

21. Needle cases   22. Ear ornaments   23. Hair ornament

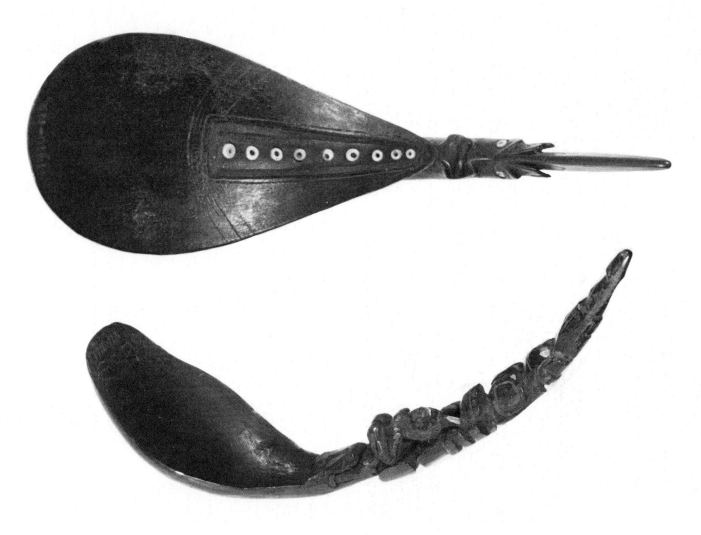

24.   Spoons

25. Spear thrower

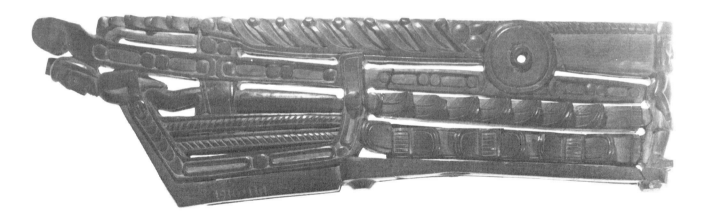

27. Pipe

26. Pipe

28. Rattle basket

29. Harpoon

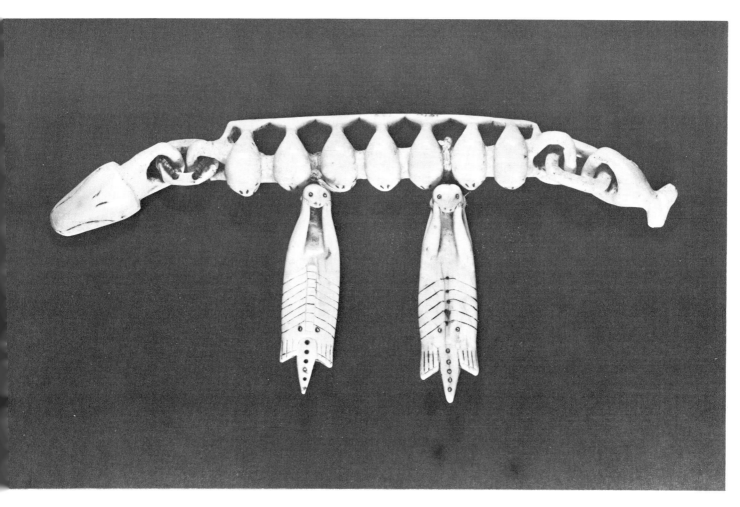

30. Ivory ornament

31. Shirt

32. Jacket

33. Hunting bag

35. Pouch

34. Bag

38.   Pipe

42.   Pipe bag

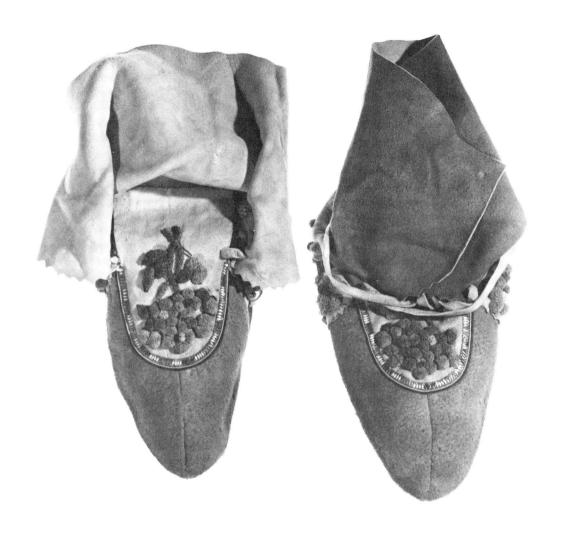

39.   Moccasins

40. Moccasins

Plate IV Unfinished mitten (cat. no. 36)

Plate V Birch bark boxes (cat. no. 37)

Plate VI Pouch (cat. no. 43)

Plate VII Pouch (cat. no. 45)

41.   Dish

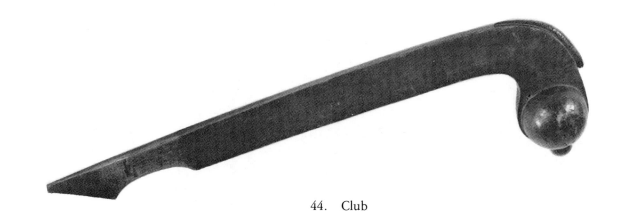

44.   Club

49.   Model canoe

46. Birch bark container

47. Cigar or tobacco box

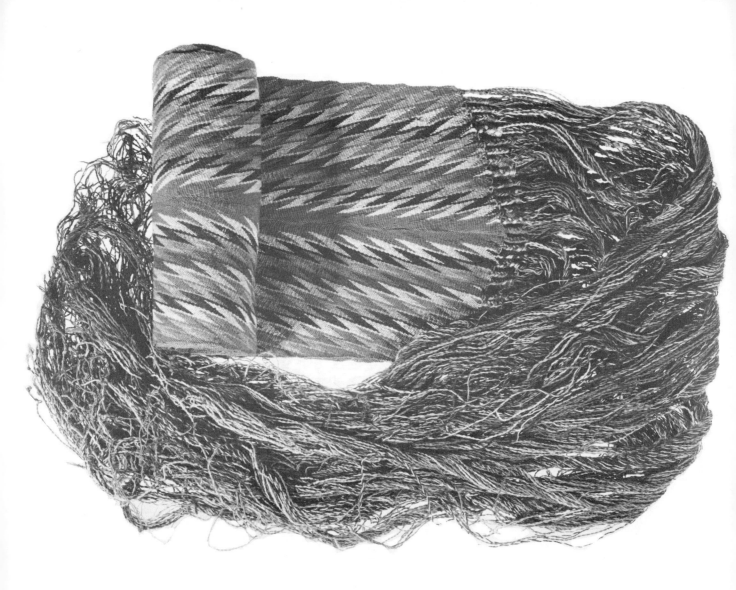

48. Sash

51.   Headdress

52. Beaded cuff

56. Single moccasins

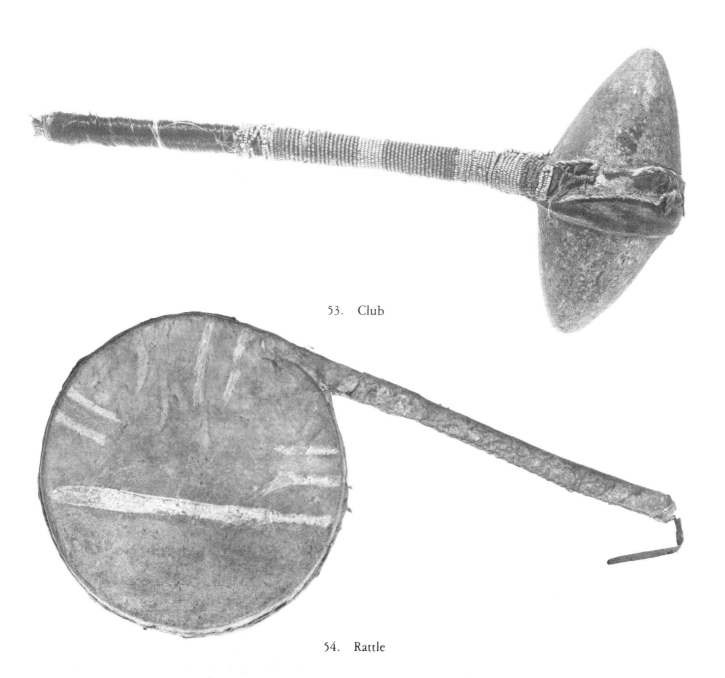

53. Club

54. Rattle

55. Bag

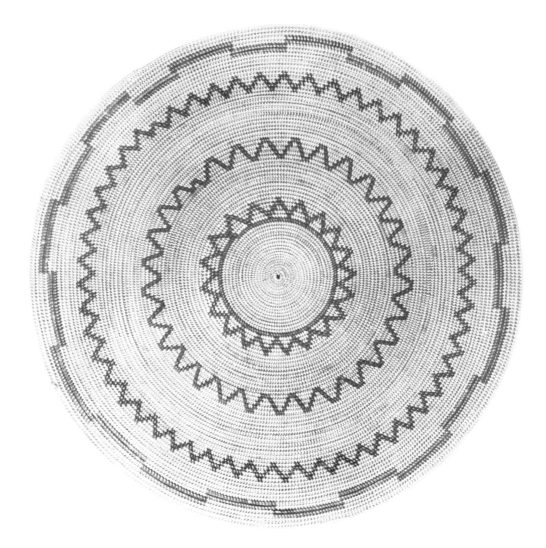

57.   Gambling tray

58.   Treasure basket

59.   Carrying basket

60.   Ladle dipper

61.   Cradleboard

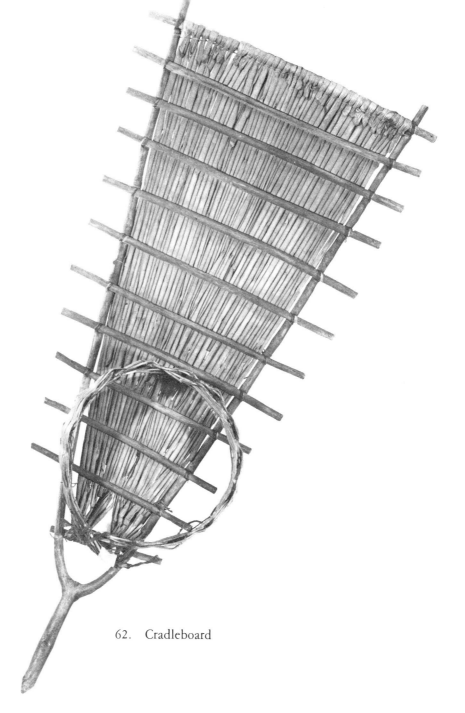

62. Cradleboard

63. Water carrier

64. Storage basket

66. Hat

65. Hat

67. Bean pot

68. Hat

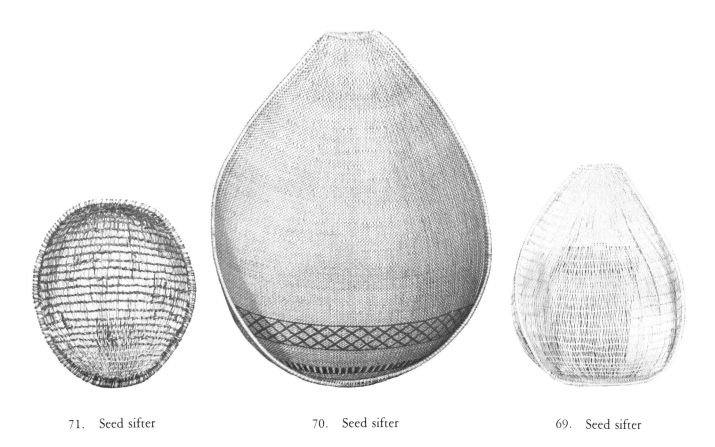

71. Seed sifter   70. Seed sifter   69. Seed sifter

72. Quill head band

a.   b.

73.   Hats

74.   Bottleneck basket

75. Feather cloak

78. Food basket

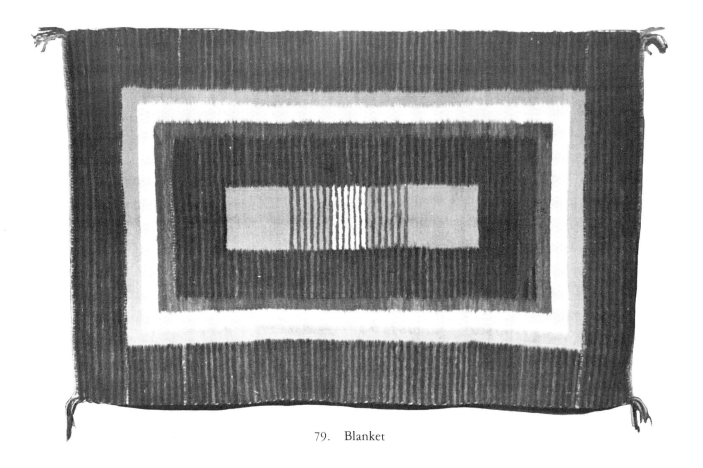

79.   Blanket

80.   Beaded boots

74

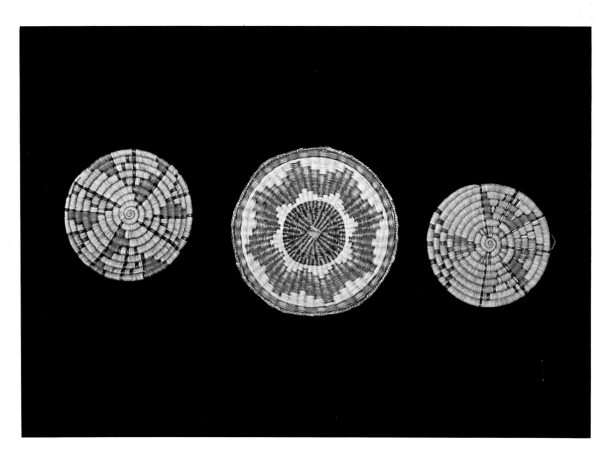

Plate VIII (l. and r.) Hopi sacred plaques (cat. no. 76); (centre)
Oraibi sacred plaque (cat. no. 77)

Plate IX Mohave dolls (cat. no. 82)

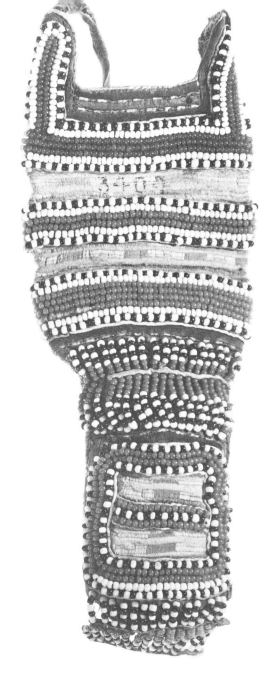

81.   Pouch

Section II:
Unillustrated Specimens

Footwear

83. MOCCASIN (23cm.)
Black-dyed deerskin moccasin beautifully embroidered with moosehair and bound with pink satin. The leather is in poor condition.
Woodlands, probably Huron.
C7:1977

84. MOCCASINS (26cm.)
Soft deerskin moccasins with high serrated ankle flaps. The insteps are decorated with three narrow rows of red, green and white quill embroidery.
Woodlands.
Thomson Coll. 1910:208

85. MOCCASINS (25cm.)
Black-dyed deerskin moccasins with heels and instep heavily decorated with ornate floral patterns in moosehair embroidery. The edges are bound with purple silk.
Grainger Coll. 3509

86. MOCCASINS (22cm.)
Dressed leather moccasins with ankle flap and red and green cloth band around heel. The insteps are decorated with orange, green and white quillwork in a geometric design reminiscent of Arapaho decorative style.
Rocky Mountains.
Donation by Mr. S. Castanin to B.N.H. & P.S. in 1843. C10:1977

87. MOCCASINS (25cm.)
Dressed leather moccasins with scalloped ankle flap edged with white beads. The edges are trimmed with black silk and the instep is of red flannel edged with white, pink and blue beads. The central design is floral and scroll patterns composed of blue, brown, yellow, pink and transparent beads.
Probably Subarctic.
Thomson Coll. donated 1843. 1910:205

88. MOCCASINS (25cm.)
Dressed leather moccasins with a strip of black cloth round the heel, ornamented with bands of red cloth trimmed with pink beads and little groups of white beads. The black cloth instep is edged with pink beads and the centre ornamented with scroll patterns in blue, pink, red, white and yellow beads.
Woodlands or Subarctic.
Donation Dr. J. D. Marshall. 1910:248

89. MOCCASINS (24cm.)
Dressed leather moccasins with long ankle flaps. A strip of red cloth runs round the heel and the insteps are of black cloth with a double scroll pattern in red cloth, edged with white beads.
Woodlands.
Thomson Coll. 1910:207

90. MOCCASINS (27cm.)
Dressed leather moccasins with long ankle flaps. The ankle is trimmed with a serrated-edge black cloth band and the insteps have silk and quill embroidery.
Mackenzie River, Canada.
1919:P73

91. MOCCASINS (25cm.)
Dressed leather moccasins with long ankle flaps and insteps decorated in floral beadwork of pink, red,

blue, yellow and two shades of green beads. Probably **fairly** modern, c.1910.
Woodlands.
C11:1977

92.   MOCCASINS (22cm.)
Dressed buckskin moccasins with ribbonwork and silk embroidered insteps. Probably fairly recent.
Woodlands.
C12:1977

93.   MOCCASINS (26cm.)
Dressed leather moccasins with long ankle flap with serrated edge. **The** apron fronts are decorated with floral silk embroidery. c.1920.
C13:1977

94.   MOCCASINS (26cm.)
Deerskin moccasins with long serrated edged ankle flaps, their insteps completely covered with geometric patterns (edged with silkwork) in red, dark red, white, green, blue and transparent beads. c.1920.
C14:1977

95.   MOCCASINS (14cm.)
Small cloth-lined buckskin moccasins. The ankle cuffs are of velvet edged with two rows of white beads. The ties of green braid and the pink cloth insteps are heavily embroidered with a coarsely worked pattern in white, blue, and transparent yellow beads.
C15:1977

96.   MOCCASINS (30cm.)
Dressed leather moccasins with long canvas ankle flaps edged with maroon cloth and decorated with strips of maroon cloth and white, green, yellow and red beads. The insteps are of black velvet edged with red silk outlined with rows of white, red, blue and green beads while the centre instep is embroidered with floral and

scroll pattern beadwork in green, red, orange, yellow, blue, pink and white.
C16:1977

97.   SINGLE MOCCASIN (24cm.)
Dressed leather moccasin with long serrated edge ankle flap. The instep is beautifully embroidered and edged with silk.
Woodlands.
C17:1977

98.   MOCCASINS (13cm.)
Baby moccasins with long ankle flaps and ties, their insteps edged with silk braid.
C18:1977

99.   MOCCASINS (24cm.)
Dressed leather moccasins with long ankle flaps. The insteps are embroidered with floral designs in silk.
C19:1977

100.   MOCCASINS (17cm.)
Dressed leather moccasins. The toe pieces are decorated right down to the edge with a shaped red cloth appliqué pattern edged with fairly large white beads. One moccasin has blue stitching in a V-shaped pattern in the middle.
Probably Woodlands.
Donated by Mr. Beck 1835. 1910:249

101.   MOCCASINS (21cm.)
Dressed leather moccasins with black velvet ankle cuffs and black cloth insteps heavily embroidered with floral beadwork in blue, pink, red, green, yellow and opaque and transparent white beads.
Woodlands.
Grainger Coll. 3432

102. MOCCASINS (25cm.)
Dressed leather moccasins with the beadwork decoration on the instep unfinished and the paper pattern underneath still attached.
Mackenzie River, Canada. 1898.
P79:1919

103. MOCCASINS (24cm.)
Dressed leather moccasins with long ankle flaps, the entire toe piece covered with geometric bead ornament in broad bands of white, green, pink, yellow, black and red. Fairly recent, c.1920.
Possibly Plains.
C20:1977

104. SINGLE MOCCASIN (24cm.)
In poor condition. The paper pattern underneath the beadwork has been cut out of an old French newspaper.
Probably Woodlands.
C21:1977

105. MOCCASINS (23cm.)
Dressed leather moccasin with serrated ankle flaps. The heels and insteps are heavily decorated with pink, red, purple, green and blue beads in floral patterns. The apron front is made of red woollen cloth, edged with a row of silk embroidery.
Woodlands, c.1920.
C22:1977

106. CHILDREN'S MOCCASINS (11cm.)
Two pairs of tiny moccasins with rawhide soles and Plains style lazy stitch beadwork on toes and round foot edge.
Donation Lord Dunleath. 1935:594

107. BOOT
Seamless boot made from the leg skin of the moose.
Thomson Coll. 1846. 1910:282

Headgear

108. UN-MADE GLENGARRY (28cm. long)
Three black velvet panels completely covered with floral bead embroidery in white, yellow, pink, red, green and blue. They are unlined but the three stitched together would have produced a native version of the Scottish Glengarry bonnet.
Huron/Iroquois.
C6:1977

109. HAT (7.5cm. hgt., 18.5cm. diam.)
Beautifully made hat in upright coil weave. The fabric is cactus bark and the colours are cream with three rows of diamond pattern at the rim and one brown band at the crown containing cream diamonds.
'Laughing Jack's Mother of Saline (Valley).'
de la Cour Carroll Coll. LCC19

110. HAT (15cm. hgt., 20cm. diam.)
Large high-crowned hat in coarse upright weave with band of treble lozenge patterns in brown at rim and crown. The crown is finished off with a little knot of red cloth.
'George Creek Squaw.'
de la Cour Carroll Coll. 13:1946

111. HAT (14.5cm. hgt., 22.5cm. diam.)
Large upright coil weave hat with four rows of lozenges on brown background round the rim. A further band of double lozenges on brown completes the decoration at the crown which is finished with a central scrap of red wool.
de la Cour Carroll Coll. LCC20

112.   HAT (13.5cm. hgt., 22 cm. diam.)
Very large hat of upright coil weave with lattice decoration at rim and crown. Its label says the decoration is burned into the straw. The preceding three hats are of very similar manufacture to this example and are probably the work of the same basketmaker.
de la Cour Carroll Coll. 14:1946

113.   HAT (12cm. hgt., 20.5cm. diam.)
Coil woven hat with broad band of rattlesnake pattern in brown and black below rim.
'Bought from Lucy Chapo camp. Lucy, last of the Monachi, daughter of Uhabe of Monache. It is not Lucy's own work.'
de la Cour Carroll Coll. 2:1946

114.   HAT (7cm. hgt., 43cm. diam.)
Large coil woven hat with shallow crown and broad rim. Brown chevron on crown and rim.
'Caroline Indians 1902.'
de la Cour Carroll Coll. 79:1946

115.   HAT (21.5cm., 11.5cm. hgt.)
Coil woven hat with five units of lightning pattern in black.
'From Sallie, daughter of last Chief of George Creek Indians.'
de la Cour Carroll Coll. 1:1946

116.   HAT (12cm. hgt., 21cm. diam.)
Coil woven hat with double running chevron design at base and rim in black.
de la Cour Carroll Coll. LCC 21

117.   HAT (11cm. hgt., 20.5cm. diam.)
Coil woven hat with treble running chevron designs at rim.
'Darwin Squaw.'
de la Cour Carroll Coll. 10:1946

118.   HAT (10.5cm. hgt., 19cm. diam.)
Coil woven hat with six groups of lightning pattern in black and one piece of lightning pattern done by mistake.
'Darwin Indian.'
de la Cour Carroll Coll. 8:1946

119.   HAT (11cm. hgt., 19.5cm. diam.)
Coil woven hat with six units of stepped pattern in brown.
'Given to me by Mr. Wilcomb.'
de la Cour Carroll Coll. 7:1946

120.   HAT (10cm. hgt., 20cm. diam.)
Coil woven hat with five units of vertical arrowhead pattern in brown and black.
'Sallie of Independence.'
de la Cour Carroll Coll. 12:1946

121.   HAT (10cm. hgt., 21cm. diam.)
Coil woven hat with five step patterns in brown bordered by parallel black lines.
'Darwin Squaw.'
de la Cour Carroll Coll. 3:1946

122.   HAT (8.5cm. hgt., 21cm. diam.)
Coil woven hat with lightning pattern of solid brown in five units. Rim and base damaged or worn.
de la Cour Carroll Coll. 6:1946

123.   HAT (11cm. hgt., 22cm. diam.)
Very attractive coil woven basket with unusual decoration. There are four vertical bands of diverging black arrowheads bordering a W design in brown and one much narrower parallel sided brown arrow design bordered in black.
'Got from Lucy of Chapo Camp, one of the last Monachis. She was given it by a Darwin squaw, mother of Thomas.'   de la Cour Carroll Coll. LCC 22

124.   HAT (9.5cm. hgt., 21cm. diam.)
Coil woven hat with inverted arrow design in brown and black.
'Independence Sally, but not made by her.'
de la Cour Carroll Coll. LCC 23

125.   HAT (12cm. hgt., 20cm. diam.)
Coil woven basket hat with three row lozenge design in brown at the rim.
'Bought from Lucy Chapo Camp. Lucy C, last of the Monachi, daughter of Uhabe of Monache, not his make.'
de la Cour Carroll Coll. 4:1946

126.   MAN'S HAT (8cm. hgt., 30cm. diam.)
Coil woven hat with broad brim.
de la Cour Carroll Coll. LCC 25

127.   SOMBRERO (35cm. diam.)
Coil woven hat, crown missing.
'Bought from Jose Lopez.'
de la Cour Carroll Coll. 59:1946

Ornaments

128.   ORNAMENT
Ornament made from the horny protuberance on the bear's paw strung on a piece of hide.
W. A. Green Coll. C1:1977

129.   CHARM
Charm made from single bear's claw strung on piece of string which has been threaded through several transparent beads.
W. A. Green Coll. C4:1977

130.   HAIR DECORATION
Six eagle feathers bound with red woollen cloth and joined together at one end.
C5:1977

131.   ORNAMENT (20cm.)
Spoon-shaped flat ornament formed of two pieces of bark sewn together and embroidered in dyed moose hair in floral patterns. A tuft of moose hair dyed white hangs from the broad end while a suspension hole has been pierced at the top of the narrow end.
Woodlands, mid-nineteenth century.
Grainger Coll. 1252

132.   ORNAMENT (9.5cm.)
Circular ornament of two round pieces of birch bark, each side ornamented with different floral patterns in moose hair embroidery. Two silk ribbon bows are tied at each side.
Grainger Coll. 1251

133.   BEADED BAND (27cm.)
Beaded band composed of a woven design of dark blue and white triangles.
Possibly Ojibwa
C26:1977

134.   LABRETS (4-6cm.)
Four elliptical wooden labrets of various sizes for fitting into a slit in the lower lip. Girls began to wear these on reaching puberty, increasing the size as time passed.
Nootka Sound, Vancouver Island
Thomson Coll. 1910:324

135.   ORNAMENT (16cm. diam.)
Circular ornament covered overall with white beadwork incorporating red and pink triangular designs interspersed with four green crosses with red centres.

The beadwork is bound with red silk and the outside edge is composed of several overlapping rows of small bird feathers. C56:1977

136. MASK (22.5cm.)
Hawk mask of natural coloured wood with black eyebrows and eyes which are unperforated. The mouth and nostrils are red. Since the eyes in this mask have not been pierced, it suggests that it was made as a trade object. Northwest Coast. The mask was unfortunately stolen from the Museum while on exhibition in September 1977.
Thomson Coll. 1910:61

Other Clothing

137. DECORATED PANEL (26cm.)
Black dyed deerskin finely decorated with a floral pattern of orange, blue and white moose hair. One edge is trimmed with a row of orange and blue dyed moosehair tassels bound with metal trade jingles.
Subarctic.
Grainger Coll. 1277

138. SOCKS AND ONE WOOL GLOVE
Rust-coloured socks and one cream glove said to have been woven by Northwest Coast Indians.
Thomson Coll. 1915:36

139. INTESTINES
Intestines of sea lion prepared for the manufacture of waterproof dresses.
Northwest Coast.
Thomson Coll. 1910:196

140. JACKET
Jacket of dressed deerskin with fringe round shoulders and chest, down both sleeves and both side seams. The shoulders, cuffs, one pocket and front panel are covered with floral beadwork of high quality in two shades of blue, two shades of green, light and dark red, pink, white, yellow and transparent beads. Although modern, the beadwork designs are beautifully executed.
Probably Subarctic. C39-1977

Cradles

141. WOODEN CRADLE (57cm.)
Cradle cut from a solid piece of cedar wood with inside sloping upwards towards the head end. Cradles like this with flaps of wood attached to the head end were used by the Northwest Coast tribes to flatten the foreheads of babies. Head-binding was also practised.
Thomson Coll. 1910:11

Many North American tribes such as the Salish, Kutenai, Natchez and Chocktaw practised head deformation as a sign of beauty or as in the case of the Northwest Coast tribes, a mark of the freeborn.

142. CRADLE (54cm.)
Small flat cradle board with rounded ends made of a fairly strong branch bent round. The body is made of straight pieces of cane while the fastening strips are made of hide and cloth. Red cloth has been struck round the edge.
Havasupai, California.
Mrs. M. Gordon C34:1977

Models

143. CANOE (42cm.)
Well-finished model canoe the edges strengthened with wooden splints sewn on and decorated with green, violet and white quillwork. The dyes seem to be vegetal colours.
Probably Micmac.
Nevin Bequest. 278:1920

144. CANOE (40cm.)
Well made model canoe with the edges strengthened by sewn on wooden splints. The sides are decorated with white, red, yellow and green quillwork.
C32:1977

145. CANOE (51cm.)
Model has been broken at either end but it is unusual in that the two ends are laced together with blue silk ribbon. Ornamented on both sides with black and yellow quillwork.
Grainger Coll. 1285

146. CANOE (39cm.)
Model of canoe carved in cedarwood with totemic decoration at either end.
Nootka Sound.
Thomson Coll. 1910:1176

Boxes

147. WORK BOX (15.5cm. diam., 12cm. hgt.)
Hexagonal bark container with circular lid. Each base panel is painted with a simple red or blue flower while the lid is decorated with a panel of white deerskin covered with floral silk embroidery. The interior is lined with violet material. Probably fairly modern.
Woodlands. C31:1977

148. BOX (7.5cm. x 5cm. x 6cm. high)
Rectangular wooden box covered with bark decorated with diagonal quillwork in blue, tan or yellow and white. The top is flat. Colours from vegetal dyes.
Micmac.
Grainger Coll. 1252

149. BOX (18cm. x 14.5cm. x 11.5cm. high)
Rectangular box with slightly domed lid. The box is of wood covered with bark decorated with blue, tan or yellow and white quillwork. The pattern on the lid is formed of triangles, circles and squares. Colours from vegetal dyes.
Micmac.
Grainger Coll. 1252

150. BOX (18.5cm. hgt.)
Cylindrical birch bark container, the top lid and base strengthened by means of wooden splints which have been sewn on. Appliqué cut-outs in floral shape have been stitched on as decoration.
H. Conn donation. C55:1977

Bags

151. BEADED BAG (16.8cm.)
Black velvet bag, bound with red cloth and decorated with simple floral pattern in blue, transparent, two shades of green, red and pink beads. There is a different floral design on each side. Brown corded handle.
Grainger Coll. 3595

152. BEADED BAG (21.5cm.)
Lozenge-shaped black velvet bag bound with red cloth and decorated with floral patterns in yellow, pink, white and green beads. Grainger Coll. 3396

153. FIRE BAG (22cm.)
This small black velvet pouch is catalogued as a fire bag. It is prettily decorated with floral bead patterns of differing design on either side in transparent and opaque pink, light and dark blue, green and transparent beads. The drawstring top has a leather thong threaded through a red velvet band.
Subarctic. Mackenzie River, 1898.
Donation Rev. A. S. Woodward. C8:1977

154. WATCH POCKET (11.5cm.)
Heart-shaped bead decorated black cloth pouch, trimmed with blue cloth and white beads. The interior is lined with tartan cloth. A woollen pompom is attached to the top. The beadwork is in the colours of pink, orange, blue, green and metal now rusted.
Fort Simpson, Mackenzie River, 1898.
Donation Rev. A. S. Woodward. C9:1977

155. BIRCH BARK BAG (21cm.)
Flat, truncated heart-shaped bag of two panels of birch bark, edged with a kind of thick grass sewn on in rows. One side is decorated with fairly simple flowers embroidered in quill. One of these flowers looks distinctly like a thistle and as the Huron Indians used to produce velvet bead-decorated hats (see no. **108**) in imitation of the Scottish glengarry, it is possible the Scottish thistle could have been the inspiration for this design. As the Scottish regiments were present in the Great Lakes region from 1840-1870, the bag might possibly be of this date.
C30:1977

156. BAG OR CONTAINER (29cm.)
Container of birch bark with concave elliptical base, the rim strengthened with an interior wooden splint sewn on.
'Given to me by Wilcomb.' (C. P. Wilcomb, Memorial Museum, Golden Gate Park, San Francisco who was a noted collector of Californian basketry).
de la Cour Carroll Coll. 84:1946

157. BAG (19.5cm.)
Hexagonal bag of black cloth trimmed with cream silk and decorated on both sides with rows of geometric bead patterns of differing design on each side. Not typical of any decorative style. Probably made as trade object.
C23:1977

158. POUCH (18.5cm.)
Round pouch of deerskin, possibly the young of Virginia white deer, edged with buckskin fringe. Its top is formed of a band of buckskin ornamented with rows of metal trade beads, spaced in groups.
50:1977

Basketry

159. BOTTLE CASE (30cm.)
Green glass wine bottle completely enclosed in woven casing.
Northwest Coast, possibly Tlingit tribe.
de la Cour Carroll Coll. 60:1946

160. DRINKING BASKET (6.3cm.)
Small straight-sided closely woven drinking basket in false embroidery technique.
Northwest Coast.
Thomson Coll. 1910:140

161. DRINKING BASKET (8.4cm.)
Straight-sided closely woven container. False embroidery gives a chequerboard design.
Northwest Coast.
Thomson Coll. 1910:139

162.   BASKET (13.5cm. hgt.)
Twined openwork basket of spruce root with false
embroidery in orange, purple and cream.
Tlingit.
Donation Mrs. M. Gordon C29:1977

163.   SEED PLAQUE (31.5cm. diam.)
Flat plaque of coiled cane woven in pairs.
'Got from Borland Bishop.'
de la Cour Carroll Coll. 47:1946

164.   DISH (33.5cm. diam.)
Flat dish in coil weave with black diamond decoration
round rim, followed by a running chevron, the
remainder of the decoration being formed of a series
of concentric bands.
'Bought from Carrimanche Coso Family.'
de la Cour Carroll Coll. LCC 18

165.   BOWL OR FOOD BASKET (38cm. diam.)
Very large well made coil woven bowl with curved
sides. The decoration is composed of four double rows
of inverted triangles in black.
'Squaw grass. Bishop Creek but made Walkers Lake.'
de la Cour Carroll Coll. 41:1946

166.   GAMBLING TRAY (46.5cm. diam.)
Very well made coil woven wicker gambling tray with
black and brown running chevron decoration. The
remainder of the decoration is composed of concentric
black circles.
'Bought from Chapo Camp. Coso Family.'
de la Cour Carroll Coll. 83:1946

167.   BOWL (12cm. hgt., 22.5cm. diam.)
Coil woven basket with five panels of inverted arrowhead design in black.
de la Cour Carroll Coll. LCC 24.

168.   BASKET (9.8cm.)
Straight-sided basket in close twined weaving in false
embroidery technique. Described as drinking basket.
Northwest Coast.
Thomson Coll. 1910:138

169.   BASKET (12.8cm.)
Straight-sided basket in close twined weaving in false
embroidery technique. Described as drinking basket.
Northwest Coast.
Thomson Coll. 1910:137

170.   BOTTLENECK (13.5cm. diam., 10cm. high)
Beautifully made coil woven bottleneck with brown
and black decoration in stepped design.
'Bought from Popinake George's wife — Piute, from
Saline Valley, California.'
de la Cour Carroll Coll. LCC 4

171.   BOTTLENECK (13cm. diam., 9.5cm. high)
Beautiful coil woven basket with horizontal zones of
dark brown containing running chevron in cream.
'Made by Nannie. Witch. Castago Squaw.'
de la Cour Carroll Coll. LCC 5

172.   BOTTLENECK (15cm. diam., 10.8cm. high)
Very well made coil woven basket with horizontal
zones of dark brown decoration of triangles and arrowheads.
'Bought from Charlie Gun's wife. Mono tribe.'
de la Cour Carroll Coll. LCC 6

173.   BOTTLENECK (15.5cm. diam., 11.3cm. high)
Very finely made coil weave basket in cream with black
chevron decoration and triangles, and lozenges in a
band round the shoulder.
'Made by Saline Squaw (Shoshone) wife of Long Nose
Gambler.'
de la Cour Carroll Coll. 18:1946

174 BOTTLENECK (16cm. diam., 13 cm. high)
Sharply shouldered coil woven basket of excellent workmanship with black lightning pattern all round body of basket and below neck.
'Got from Nannie of Grape Vine Canyon.'
de la Cour Carroll Coll. LCC 7

175. BOTTLENECK (12.2cm. diam., 9.6cm. high)
Small globular open-neck coil woven basket with lightning pattern in black around widest part of body.
'Made by Saline Squaw. I think Patsy, wife of Thomas Chapo.'
de la Cour Carroll Coll. LCC 8

176. BOTTLENECK (18.8cm. diam., 11cm. high)
Squat bottleneck basket with fairly narrow high neck in coil weave rattlesnake pattern overall in black and reddish brown. Two rows of red wool woven in and there are also some white bird quills incorporated in the design.
'Got from Chapo's mother. Rattlesnake pattern and wool decoration. Had been in use long time.'
de la Cour Carroll Coll. 1946:16

177. BOTTLENECK (16.6cm. diam., 12.4cm. high)
Beautifully woven coil weave basket with fairly sharp shoulder in cream with dark brown lozenge pattern in three zones.
'Bought from Nannie, Witch of Castago?'
de la Cour Carroll Coll. 1946:23

178. BOTTLENECK (14.5cm. diam., 9.2cm. hgt.)
Very fine coil woven basket in cream with black zig zag round neck and what might be called quail tip pattern in three zones on body of pot.
'Bought from Currincueda, Chapo Camp. Coso family.'
Possibly Yuki tribe.
de la Cour Carroll Coll. 1946:19

179. BOTTLENECK (13.5cm. diam., 11.4cm. high)
Very fine coil woven cream coloured basket, highly patterned with vertical rows of lightning pattern, arrowheads, lozenges and two standing male figures in black.
'Bought from wife of Popinake George of Kuler-Piute tribe.'
de la Cour Carroll Coll. LCC 9

180. BOTTLENECK (14.5cm. diam., 8.8cm. high)
Very well made cream coloured coil woven basket with four vertical zones of zig zags composed of rectangles interspersed with a single cross.
'Bought from Chiphaw mother who got it Coso Way, near Death Valley.'
de la Cour Carroll Coll. 24:1946

181. TRINKET BASKET (14.8cm. diam., 15cm. high)
Necked globular basket with rounded base in twined weave with arrowhead pattern bounding two rows of running chevrons around widest part of basket, in dark brown.
Possibly Mohave workmanship.
de la Cour Carroll Coll. 1946:26

182. BOTTLENECK (13cm. diam., 9.8cm. high)
Fairly crudely made coil woven basket with rather untidy design in brown and black stepped rectangles. One row of red wool on shoulder.
Mohave Indian.
de la Cour Carroll Coll. 25:1946

183. TRINKET BASKET (13.5cm. diam., 8cm. high)
Small slightly lop-sided basket with two zones of chevron decoration in brown.
'Got from Jose Lopez wife.'
de la Cour Carroll Coll. LCC 10

184. BOTTLENECK (10.5cm. diam. of mouth, 10cm. hgt.)
Coil woven basket with design of chevron and open lozenge in black.
'Saline Valley. Made by Laughing Jack's Mother.'
de la Cour Carroll Coll. LCC 11

185. BOTTLENECK (8cm. neck diam., 15cm. body diam., 13.5cm. hgt.)
Narrow-necked basket of coil weave with brown chevron at base and at greatest circumference. A row of nine male figures in brown is woven round the base.
May be of Apache workmanship.
de la Cour Carroll Coll. 20:1946

186. BOTTLENECK (10cm. diam., 10cm. hgt.)
Coil woven basket, the decoration composed of two rows of deer in brown.
'Got from Jose Lopez woman. Made by Darwin squaw.'
de la Cour Carroll Coll. 22:1946

187. BOWL (10.4cm. hgt., 23.5cm. diam.)
Attractive coil woven bowl with four vertical zones of arrow design in black, reddish brown, edged with white bird quillwork.
'Inverted arrow with quillwork.'
de la Cour Carroll Coll. LCC 12

188. BASKET (11cm. hgt., 33cm. diam.)
Coil woven basket of eight vertical rows of reddish brown fern or arrow pattern each one of which ends in two black rows.
'Hogadi basket. Bought from Mother of Popinake George, Pintitupe.'
de la Cour Carroll Coll. 40:1946

189. BASKET (14cm. hgt., 38cm. diam.)
Well made coil woven basket of cream with three zones of stepped pattern in black. These are bounded on each side by quail tip patterns. Possibly Pomo manufacture.
'Very old.'
de la Cour Carroll Coll. LCC 13

190. BOWL (7.5cm. hgt., 16cm. diam.)
Very well made coil woven bowl in cream with five double stepped patterns in black and one treble stepped pattern.
'Made by Saline Squaw, Laughing Jack's Mother.'
de la Cour Carroll Coll. LCC 14

191. BOWL (7.5cm. hgt., 18.6cm. diam.)
Beautifully made coil woven bowl with five vertical rows of black containing arrow design.
'Saline Squaw, Pete's wife. Twisted arrow.'
de la Cour Carroll Coll. LCC 15

192. BOWL (5cm. hgt., 20cm. diam.)
Bowl of coarser coil weave with two rows of either running chevron or lightning pattern in reddish brown beneath rim.
'Made by Popinase. Lone Pine Squaw.'
de la Cour Carroll Coll. LCC 16

193. STORAGE BASKET (18cm. hgt., 41cm. diam.)
Large well made coil woven basket with four zones of brown tapering solid zigzag pattern each one bordered by parallel black lines. Three formalised female figures set between each zone.
de la Cour Carroll Coll. 38:1946

194. BASKET (8cm. hgt., 42.5cm. diam.)
Large very well made basket in coil weave attractively patterned with three sets of double blunt chevrons in brown.
'Bought from Frank of Chapo Camp.'
de la Cour Carroll Coll. 39:1946

195. SEED PLAQUE (34.5cm. diam.)
Circular basket in coarse coil weave with decoration of parallel brown lines in five pairs.
'Bought at Fort Independence.'
de la Cour Carroll Coll. 46:1946

196. SEED SIFTER (26cm.)
Closely woven seed sifter the rim strengthened by a wooden splint and decorated with a row of brown zig-zags.
'Pete's Squaw. Saline Family.' i.e. Indians living in Saline Valley, California.
de la Cour Carroll Coll. LCC 26

197. SEED SIFTER (27cm.)
Closely woven scoop-shaped seed sifter.. Decoration consists of a band of chevrons and lozenges.
'Bought from Saline Squaw. Pete's wife.'
de la Cour Carroll Coll. 48:1946

198. SEED SIFTER (26.5cm.)
Open-weave shield-shaped sifter in cane.
de la Cour Carroll Coll. 50:1946

199. BASKET (11cm. hgt., 18cm. diam.)
Coarsely woven basket of fern root. The top is finished with a binding of red and white dotted cotton.
'Warm Springs Reservation, Dallas, Oregon.'
de la Cour Carroll Coll. 37:1946

200. GATHERING BAG (50cm. long)
Pliable closely woven basket, boat-shaped with double plaited carrying handles at either end.
'Hopi Indian, Arizona.'
de la Cour Carroll Coll. 63:1946

201. BOTTLE CASE (30cm.)
Green glass bottle enclosed in wicker sleeve in knotted horizontal weave.
Possibly Northwest Coast.
de la Cour Carroll Coll. 61:1946

202. SACRED PLAQUE (22cm. diam.)
Oraibi sacred wicker plate in red, green and black.
de la Cour Carroll Coll. LCC 27

203. SACRED PLAQUE (22cm. diam.)
Oraibi sacred wicker plaque in red, green and black. pattern. Worn.
de la Cour Carroll Coll. 54:1946

204. SACRED PLAQUE (26cm. diam.)
Oraibi sacred wicker plaque in green, orange and black.
de la Cour Carroll Coll. 55:1946

205. SACRED PLAQUE (43cm. diam.)
Oraibi sacred wicker plaque in green, orange, red and dark blue.
C33:1977

206. CARRYING BASKET (41cm. by 21cm. deep)
Closely woven basket in cream and brown. Four double carrying loops on rim.
Quinault Indian, Washington. 'Made by Shaker Preacher's wife.'
de la Cour Carroll Coll. 43:1946

207. GOBLET (11cm. hgt.,)
Beautifully made coil woven goblet with 'I am' and a cross in brown woven around the sides.
Probably Mission Indian.
de la Cour Carroll Coll. LCC 28

208. BASKET (17cm. hgt., 8cm.)
Small oval basket in coarse straw. Stylised figures of three men and three women round the side. The

women are woven in purplish blue and the men in black.
Maricopa.
de la Cour Carroll Coll. LCC 29

209. BOWL (13.5cm. diam., 6cm. hgt.)
Small coil woven bowl with design of stepped rectangles joining four little men in black. Much worn.
de la Cour Carroll Coll. LCC 30

210. TRINKET BASKET (11cm. diam., 6cm. hgt.)
Small bowl of coiled cane bound in pairs. Red wool has been used for decoration at the rim.
Bishop, California (home of Mono tribe).
de la Cour Carroll Coll. 34:1946

211. TRINKET BASKET (10.5cm. diam., 6cm. hgt.)
Small bowl with mouth slightly narrower than body coiled cane bound in pairs with red cloth strips woven in near rim.
Bishop, California (Mono).
de la Cour Carroll Coll. 32:1946

212. TRINKET BASKET (13cm. diam., 6.5cm. hgt.)
Small bowl of coiled cane bound in pairs with band of red wool decoration at rim.
Bishop, California.
de la Cour Carroll Coll. 33:1946

213. TRINKET BASKET (7cm. diam., 7.5cm. hgt.)
Small straight-sided container of coiled cane bound in pairs with a band of red wool decoration near rim. Rim damaged.
Probably Mono.
de la Cour Carroll Coll. 35:1946

214. TRINKET BASKET (11cm. diam., 7.5cm. hgt.)
Small bowl with incurved mouth of coiled cane bound in pairs. A row of red wool and a row of black cloth bound in the weave constitutes the decoration at the top.
de la Cour Carroll Coll. 36:1946

215. GRANARY BASKET (45cm. diam.)
Very large coiled basket or tray made of strips of bark wrapped round a grass or straw foundation. The centre is finished off with a small circle of orange cloth. The only decoration is of four very small brown rectangles forming a cross.
Southwest region, possibly Pueblo basketry.
C35:1977

216. BOWL (18cm. diam., 6.5cm. hgt.)
Basket of coarse coil weave.
'Squaw grass.'
de la Cour Carroll Coll. 30:1946

217. BOWL (20.5cm. diam., 6.5cm. hgt.)
Very beautiful conical basket in very fine coil weave. The decoration consists of vertical converging rows of fern pattern in black.
'Made by Pete's Squaw. Saline Valley.'
de la Cour Carroll Coll. LCC 17

218. STORAGE BASKET (45cm. diam., 20cm. hgt.)
Very large coil-woven wide-mouthed basket with three horizontal bands of black lozenges as decoration.
'Bought from Chapo's Mother, Coso.' i.e. Coso Valley, California.
de la Cour Carroll Coll. 44:1946

Pottery

219. BOWL (14cm. diam., 14cm. hgt.)
Shouldered bowl of low-fired cinnamon-coloured clay with concave base. The neck and shoulder are painted

white and have simple leaf-like decoration in black.
Pueblo.
Nevin Bequest 256:1920

220.   ANTHROPOMORPHIC POT (16cm. hgt.)
Low-fired pottery in reddish coloured clay with round
base. The whole pot has been covered with a white
slip, the features outlined in black. The opening is
provided by the protruding lips.
Pueblo.
C36:1977

221.   POT (8cm. hgt., 11cm. diam.)
Low-fired pot with round base in cinnamon-coloured
clay. The black, red and white painted decoration has
mostly worn away.
Pueblo.
C37:1977

222.   POT (14cm. hgt., 13cm. diam.)
Small round-based pot narrowing towards rim. The
painted decoration is in red, black and white.
C38:1977

223.   HEN (7cm. hgt.)
Round-bodied, small-headed hen with black base,
dotted with white. The head and neck are painted
reddish-brown.
Pueblo.
Grainger Coll. 1127

224.   CUP (5cm. hgt.)
Shallow cup with one handle in cinnamon-coloured
clay painted white with a band of black lozenges filled
with diagonal lines at the rim and a narrow orange
band beneath.
Grainger Coll. 1127

Amusements

225.   CIGAR OR TOBACCO BOX (8cm.)
Small rectangular birch bark container with sleeve lid
beautifully embroidered in dyed moose hair with floral
patterns. The top is unfortunately broken.
L'Estrange Garrett Coll. 386:1912

226.   PIPE (29.5cm.)
Wooden smoking pipe. Its label says it was only used
by the very old men of the Pomo tribe.
'From Bentley Ranchorin, Mendocino Co., California.'
de la Cour Carroll Coll. LCC 1

227.   PIPE (11.8cm.)
Argillite pipe with small round bowl with ribs on out-
side surface, rising from rectangular stem.
Haida, Queen Charlotte Sound, British Columbia.
Donation W. G. Byron. 645:1954

228.   PIPE (15cm.)
Long pipe of argillite carved with intertwined men and
animals. Small portion missing from one end.
Haida.
Thomson Coll. 1910:154

229.   WHISTLE (11.5cm.)
Dance whistle made from a double reed decorated
with red cloth and blue thread and hung with three
little strings of transparent beads ending in a piece of
shell.
Pomo, California.
C3:1977

230.   LEG RATTLE
Rattle composed of nut shells strung on knotted twine.
The ends of each string originally had a feather
attached but most of these are now missing.
C27:1977

231. PIPE (15cm.)
Argillite pipe carved with intertwined ravens and frogs.
Haida.
Thomson Coll. 1910:154

Tools

232. LOOM
Twig with threads attached for weaving beadwork band in dark blue and white labryinth pattern.
C24:1977

233. LOOM
Primitive loom consisting of a stick with two small twigs tied at right angles at top and bottom. On the attached threads is part of a woven bead band in white with dark blue and red star patterns.
C25:1977

234. BRUSH (5.8cm.)
Small brush used for removing traces of acorn mush from inside cooking baskets. It is made from a bunch of grasses bent over and tied round near the top.
Pomo, California.
de la Cour Carroll Coll. LCC 2

235. HALIBUT HOOK (35cm.)
Wooden hook with bone barb, carved in the shape of a lizard. Unfortunately broken and worm eaten but forms a trio with the two others illustrated (Plate **8a.** and **b.**)

236. SPOON (29.5cm.)
Wooden spoon with the head of a deer carved on the handle just above the bowl.
Northwest Coast Thomson Coll. 1910:114

237. SIDE ADZE (17cm.)
Side adze of close-grained stone.
Northwest Coast
612:1922

238. AXE (13cm.)
Close-grained polished stone axe of oval section. One end is fairly deeply waisted for the fitting of a shaft, the other narrows to an oval striking edge. Donated 1884.
1911:1053

Weapons and Miscellaneous

239. ROPE
Rope made from the inner bark of the stem of a wild plant.
Foothills of High Sierra.
C2:1977

240. SHEATH (22cm.)
Black dyed leather sheath fringed round the edge and ornately embroidered with moose hair in scroll patterns of orange, white and blue. In poor condition.
Woodlands, probably Huron.
1910:329

241. BOW (1.59m.)
Wooden bow with painted black and red decoration. Both ends have been bound with black wool and string. The bow is of the double-recurve type and is probably Modoc tribe, California. Unfortunately it has been cut in two and a hinge added for ease of transport.
de la Cour Carroll Coll. LCC 3

242.   SPEAR THROWER (46.8cm.)
Plain wooden spear thrower with piece of bone slotted
in and finger notches carved on one side.
Northwest Coast.
Steiglitz Collection c.1820. 1910:749

243.   SPOON (17cm.)
Horn spoon, the handle composed of an upside down
human figure.
Northwest Coast.
Thomson Coll. 1910:111

244.   JAVELIN (head 32cm. long, total lgth. 1.71m.)
Javelin with slender leaf-shaped wooden head spliced
to shaft and double flight of feathers at end of shaft.
The head is further held by a wrapping of very fine
twine.
Donation J. Charley. 1910:713

NOTES

1. D. Snow: *The American Indians*, p. 23.
2. S. Phelps: *Art and Artefacts of the Pacific, Africa and the Americas*, p. 306.
3. Fd. J. Dockstader: *Indian Art of the Americas*, p. 15.
4. R. Cox: *Adventures on the Columbia River*, pp. 301-3.
5. S. Phelps, *op., cit.*, p. 302.
6. S. Phelps, *op. cit.*, p. 332.
7. E. A. Barber: *American Glassware*, 1900, p. 101.
8. H. W. Kreiger: 'Aboriginal Decorative Art': *Annual Report of Smithsonian Institution* (1930), p. 548.
9. French words often occur in connection with the North American Indian. This is because many of the first European encounters with the native population were made by French trappers and explorers. For example the Nez Perce (literally pierced nose) were first visited by French Canadians in 1812 (see *The Nez Perce* by Francis Haines, University of Oklahoma Press) who were impressed by the nose ornaments worn by the tribe and the name continued to be used. Words such as parfleche and travois have similar origins.
10. Wm. Wildschut and J. C. Ewers: *Crow Indian Medicine Bundles*, p. 65.
11. S. Phelps, *op. cit.*, p. 330.
12. O. T. Mason: *Indian Basketry*, Vol. II, p. 384.
13. S. Phelps, *op. cit.*, pp. 367-371.
14. H. M. Humphreys: *Men of the time in Australia* (Melbourne, 1882), pp. 177-8.
15. A. Wilson: *Fragments that Remain*, p. 75.
16. O. T. Mason in *North American Bows, Arrows and Quivers* (Smithsonian Report, 1893) states that the sinew-corded bow was used almost exclusively by the Eskimo. His description of this type of South Alaskan bow fits the Ulster Museum example closely except that none of the illustrated bows is quite the same as the Ulster Museum one. He later quotes from Sproat's *Scenes*, on p. 47 of his own book: 'The native bow in Vancouver's Island is beautifully formed. It is generally made of yew or crab-apple wood and is 3½ ft long with about 2 inches at each end turned sharply backward from the string. The string is a piece of dried seal gut, deer sinew or twisted bark.' This description also fits the Ulster Museum bow and as Thomson was usually careful about provenances and as the bow was accompanied by three arrows, a similar one to which is illustrated by Phelps (Plate 183, No. 1515) and designated to the Tlingit of Alaska, there seems no reason to doubt that it was collected from one of the Northwest Coast tribes.
17. P. L. Macnair: Descriptive notes on the Kwakiutl manufacture of eulachon oil, *Syesis*, 4. pp. 169-77.
18. Mrs. L. Lichliter of the Smithsonian Institution, Washington comments that such Eskimo carvings would have been used as handles for wooden buckets and that the rather inconvenient pendant seal figures were probably attached at a later date. There was a permanent state of conflict between Eskimo and Indian and such an object might have arrived in Vancouver Island as part of the spoils of war.

BIBLIOGRAPHY

Boas, F. *Primitive Art*. New York, 1955.

Cox, R. *Adventures on the Columbia River*. London, 1831, 2 Vols.

Dockstader, Fd. J. *Indian Art of the Americas*. New York, 1973.

Feder, N. *200 Years of American Indian Art*. New York, 1971.

Holm, B. *Northwest Coast Indian Art*. University of Washington Press, 1965.

Inverarity, R. B. *Art of the Northwest Coast Indians* University of California Press, 1967.

Kreiger, H. W. 'Aboriginal Decorative Art': *Annual Report of Smithsonian Institution* (1930). Washington DC, 1931.

Kroeber, A. L. 'Handbook of the Indians of California': *Bureau of American Ethnology, Bulletin 78 Smithsonian Institution*. Washington DC, 1924.

McKenny, Thos. L. *and* Hall, J. *The Indian Tribes of North America*. Published in 1836 and republished in 1933-4. Yorkshire, 1972 reprint, 3 Vols.

Mason, O. T. *Indian Basketry*. New York, 1904, 2 vols.

————— *North American Bows, Arrows and Quivers*. Smithsonian Report, 1893.

Orchard, Wm. C. *Beads and Beadwork of the American Indian*. Museum of the American Indian. New York, 1975.

Phelps, S. *Art and Artefacts of the Pacific, Africa and the Americas*. The James Hooper Collection, London, 1976.

Snow, D. *The American Indians*. London, 1976.

Swanton, Dr. J. R. 'Indian Tribes of the Lower Mississippi Valley and the Adjacent Coast of the Gulf of Mexico': *Bureau of American Ethnology, Bulletin 43, Smithsonian Institution*. Washington DC, 1911.

Wildschut, Wm. *and* Ewers, J. C. *Crow Indian Medicine Bundles*. Museum of the American Indian, New York, 1975.

ACKNOWLEDGEMENTS

I wish to thank the following individuals and organisations, who have helped to make this book possible: the Trustees and Director of the Ulster Museum for their permission to produce this book; L. N. W. Flanagan, Keeper of Antiquities for constant assistance throughout the production of the book; W. Porter, Senior Photographer, Ulster Museum, for all the photographic plates; A. H. Eveleigh, Ulster Museum, for the design of the book; Mrs. Deirdre Crone, Antiquities Department, Ulster Museum, for the drawings of the cover design from a Northwest Coast legging and the map; C. D. Deane, formerly Deputy Director, Ulster Museum, R. Nash, P. Hackney and Mrs. H. Ross of the Natural Sciences Department for identifying bird feathers, shells and wood used in specimens; Dr. B. G. Scott, J. G. Kelly, H. G. Murray and Wilma Harper for repair and conservation of some important specimens; Mrs. R. Whitehead of Nova Scotia Museum, Canada for much helpful information on birch bark ornament and quill embroidery; J. C. H. King of the Museum of Mankind, Ethnography Department of the British Museum for helpful discussion; J. and Diane Gracey for advice; Mrs. P. Tricker who typed the manuscript and P. Glover for constant encouragement. Special thanks are due to Miss M. Scott Rooney who assisted with many interesting details about G. A. Thomson and I am also most grateful to Mr. A. W. K. Colmer of the Lecale Historical Society for information on A. W. de la Cour Carroll.

Winifred Glover